youth netball 101 *drills*

age **12** to **16**

Also available from A & C Black

101 Youth Soccer Drills – Age 7–11
2nd edition
Malcolm Cook

101 Youth Soccer Drills – Age 12–16
2nd edition
Malcolm Cook

101 Youth Netball Drills – Age 7–11
Anna and Chris Sheryn

101 Youth Hockey Drills
Stuart Dempster and Dennis Hay

anna and chris sheryn

youth netball

101 *drills*

age **12** to **16**

A & C Black • London

Published in 2005 by
A & C Black Publishers Ltd
37 Soho Square
London W1D 3QZ
www.acblack.com

ISBN 0 7136 7195 5

A CIP catalogue record for this book is available from the British Library.

Acknowledgements
Cover illustration by Alex Williamson
Textual illustrations by Q2A Solutions
Photographs on p. 6, p. 86 and p. 94 courtesy of Getty Images
Photographs on p. 28 and p. 114 courtesy of Action Images

Note: While every effort has been made to ensure that the content of this book is as technically accurate and as sound as possible, neither the authors nor the publishers can accept responsibility for any injury or loss sustained as a result of the use of this material.

A & C Black uses paper produced with elemental chlorine-free pulp, harvested from managed sustainable forests.

Typeset in 10/12pt DIN regular
Printed and bound in Great Britain by The Cromwell Press, Trowbridge, Wiltshire

CONTENTS

ACKNOWLEDGEMENTS

Thank you to my enthusiastic guinea pigs at Ashgate Netball Squad and all the children at Cowling Primary School Netball Club. Also, thank you to all those coaches of netball training sessions I have enjoyed over the years, from school to county.

INTRODUCTION

This book is designed to provide coaches, teachers and parents with a resource to construct effective drill sessions for young netballers. While it is more than likely that players in the 12–16 age group will demonstrate a high level of playing competence, it is a common mistake to treat them as 'mini adults'. Their experience of netball in these most important of years can determine whether or not they continue to play (at any level) into adult life and can influence their view of sport in general.

The key objective of any training session with this age group is to ensure that the players will want to come back for the next one. They must feel that they have progressed, learned something new, and, most importantly, had a good time! This book will provide coaches with ideas for varied and structured training sessions that will allow players to develop the whole range of skills needed to become a good netballer, including ball skills, attacking, defending and shooting. Each drill contains coaching points to help make each session more effective, and ideas to progress the drill to ensure players remain interested.

KEY TO DIAGRAMS

GS	Goal Shooter
GA	Goal Attack
WA	Wing Attack
C	Centre
WD	Wing Defence
GD	Goal Defence
GK	Goal Keeper
△	cones
- - - - - - - -►	movement of ball
———►	movement of player

SESSION GUIDELINES

buying in

It is important that the players are well aware of the objectives behind each activity. This 'buying in' is doubly important when explaining the more abstract and complex drills, as unless the players understand why they are being asked to do something, they will not totally engage themselves in the activity. This is especially vital for young players, who will not be experienced enough to understand why all this running about is going to help their game.

When you introduce a drill, ensure that everyone is very clear on:

- the skill they are practising: 'this drill focuses on running to receive a pass head-on'
- why it is an important skill: 'you can use this skill to drive towards the pass in a game and therefore beat your marker to the ball'
- what a good job looks like: 'get your hands up early as you run, then cushion the ball in as you take the pass; start slowly for the first few passes, then gradually build up speed and see what your limits are'
- mistakes are positive: practice and drills are the place to try things out. For example, 'How far can you hang back from your marker (to draw the pass) and still manage to get the interception?' Until players 'fail', they cannot measure their limits and then work to improve on them. Always congratulate players who are trying as well as those who succeed.

building drills

When you are introducing complex drills to groups of players, always explain each element separately so that everyone is clear about what they have to do before they start. By flooding the group with information, you run the risk of the drill becoming disorganised or falling apart. For example, if the drill involves a run–receive–land–pass sequence, demonstrate and describe the run and land only at first so that everyone can see and understand what a good job looks like. Only add the next element when the basics are spot on. There is absolutely no point in introducing a ball to a drill if the running and landing principle is not understood.

quality before quantity

Building an environment of excellence can be achieved without becoming boring. Just be very clear and concise about the skills you are about to practise and then concentrate on quality of execution at all times. Do not be drawn into lengthy drills that test stamina and reduce quality of play – short, sharp, top-quality drills will ensure that top-quality play is ingrained.

Remember: 'Practice does not make perfect; it makes permanent.' If sloppiness is part of the training regime, it will become ingrained in performances.

the learning curve

The development of a skill during a group practice will not follow a straight line. It is usual for awareness and concentration initially to be high, and for skills to develop at a corresponding rate. However, as the drill progresses concentration levels will fall and therefore so will players' accuracy. If this is allowed to continue unchecked by the coach, competency levels will suffer.

To address this issue, coaches must constantly be aware of the pattern of the players' concentration levels and take time to rest their minds and bodies. Stop the drill, re-communicate the objective and the skills involved and then, once the players are rested and ready – both mentally and physically – start again. In this way the inevitable decline in competency can be arrested and the development curve can be edged upwards.

confidence

When boys encounter problems they are likely to blame the ball, the weather, the passer – anything but themselves. With girls, the first port of call tends to be their own performance. This means that the coach must ensure that confidence is not undermined by progressing drills too quickly for the ability of the players. Instead, use drills that provide initial success, and progress slowly. Always focus on what has gone right and not on perceived failures.

communication

In any sport, on most training nights you will see a coach struggling to form young players into pre-drill formations. Instructions such as 'Get into a circle' or 'I need two staggered lines' result in formations that owe more to a stage farce than a netball session. This leads to exasperated coaches, confused players and wasted time.

Never fear – here are some tips to help you overcome some common problems.

Watch your language

I know an excellent tennis coach who, when working with a group of 6–8-year-olds, told them to 'Stand in the tramlines'. I mentioned to him afterwards that the reason that not all of them responded was that many of them had no idea what a tramline was, and even less idea which area of the court he was talking about.

Try at all times to take account of the age and experience of your players before you speak. Avoid jargon like the plague, explain what you mean and constantly question and re-evaluate your use of language. If you want to test yourself, ask a non-netballer to watch a session and keep a list of all the terms that they do not understand. Have a look at the list and then ask yourself what you really meant!

'Get into pairs/groups of three etc.'

You can pair up older players by asking everyone to put their hands in the air and keep them there until they have a partner. In this way it is easier for everyone to see who remains.

'Make a circle'

Ask a group of players (of almost any age) to form a circle, and what you get will likely resemble a football crowd. A good way to achieve an evenly spaced circle is to ask all the players to hold hands and then slowly walk backwards as far as they can without letting go. You will be left with an evenly spaced circle.

'Form a staggered line'

In a number of the drills in this book you will need the players to form two parallel lines in a zigzag formation. This, again, can be a real struggle. The easy way to do this is in four steps:

1. Ask the players to form a single line and then hold hands.
2. Spread them out until they can only just hold onto each other – they will then be evenly spaced.
3. Number alternate players one and two – 'One, two, one, two' etc.
4. All number ones stand still. All number twos walk out to form the second line. When both lines turn to face each other, they will form the perfect 'zigzag'.

warming up

A 'warm-up' is necessary to prepare the body for exercise but, contrary to traditional wisdom, there is no evidence that stretching *before* exercise improves performance or reduces the risks of injury. Instead, stretches should be performed *after* exercise.

In comparison, a warm-up should consist of similar movements to the exercises players are about to perform. There is no point running around the court for ten minutes if you are then going to perform a series of sprints or jumps. Think about the range of movements that you are preparing the players for and gradually build up the intensity from gentle warm-up to near-performance level.

Be careful not to warm-up for too long to avoid using up energy that should be reserved for playing. Players will need to sweat a little, but shouldn't be fatigued by the warm-up. A good rule of thumb is to elevate the heart rate to the extent that players are sweating lightly and are mildly out of breath.

warming down

This is a much ignored area of coaching sessions. The last five minutes (at least) of a session should be given over to warming down. This can be done by simply running slowly once around the court followed by two or three stretching drills (see Chapter 8) and a slow jog or walk around the court to finish.

As mentioned above, the warm-down is the place to work on flexibility, and if stretches are carried out consistently players should not experience stiffness in the days following practice or matches. Following exercise the soft tissues will be warm and as a result their inherent ability to stretch will be increased, so any attempts to increase basic flexibility should be carried out in this period. For example, if players have one or two areas that they know are tight (such as the hamstrings or calf muscles), it would be sensible to specifically target these areas with stretches during the warm-down.

drill categories

The drills in this book are divided into the following categories:

1 Warming up
2 Ball skills (passing and catching)
3 Movement and footwork
4 Attacking and defending
5 Shooting
6 Conditioned games
7 Warming down

session structure

There are as many ways to compile a session as there are coaches. There are, however, some basic guidelines that will help a session make sense for players and coaches alike. A one-hour session might look like this:

1 Warm-up (10 minutes): while this is taking place, let the players know what the objective is for the session and – most importantly – why this objective is important. (For example, 'We are going to spend some time practising driving onto the pass, as this will reduce the number of interceptions we give away in a match.)
2 Drills (25 minutes): these should be taken from the sections that cover ball skills, movement and footwork, attacking and defending and shooting. Try to focus on one common skill even if you are covering more than one topic so that everyone is clear at the end of the session what has been learned.
3 Conditioned Games (15 minutes): these involve plenty of fun and require lots of energy. Only stop the action when the key skills need to be reaffirmed and some order returned.
4 Warming down (10 minutes): don't skimp on this section. Young players will have less need for flexibility development than adult players but warming-down is an invaluable habit to get into. The warm-down is also a great opportunity to reaffirm what has just been practised and reiterate key learning points. For example, 'We've just seen the value of driving onto the ball in the conditioned game and learned how communication makes the job that much easier.'

Players of all ages have one thing in common – they prefer playing to practising. With this in mind, make sure that sessions are fun. A sense of humour on court is essential as it not only keeps the coach sane, but also removes the tension that can make players less inclined to extend themselves and risk mistakes.

Notice how Fiona Dovan (the Phoenix, Australia) uses her body to keep the ball away from the defender and is looking for the next pass.

WARMING UP

As previously mentioned, the warm-up is an important part of the session. While there is no evidence to prove that a warm-up aids performance or helps to avoid injuries, experience tells us that a relevant and focused warm-up prepares both mind and body for the practice. The warm-up is also an opportunity for the players to weigh up a new coach, so if you are new to the group make sure that your session is well planned, clear, well delivered and, above all, fun!

Contrary to traditional wisdom, the warm-up is not the place to improve flexibility (save this for the warm-down when the muscles are warm). The warm-up should be controlled and replicate the types of activities that you will be focusing on in the body of the session. So, three times around the court then touch your toes is not really what we are after!

The following drills provide some ideas for warming up with and without the ball. Always follow the same rule – build speed and intensity gradually and focus on quality of movement at all times.

Objective: To develop foot speed, balance and control of movement.

Equipment: Cones.

Description: Set up a line of cones 5 m away from the side line. The players stand on the side line facing the cones then, using very fast feet and tiny steps, move towards the cones. When the players reach the cones they turn and walk slowly back to the side line and start again. The objective is to complete as many tiny steps in the shortest amount of time possible.

Coaching points: Youngsters will lose concentration and form very quickly and will increase the length of their steps in order to move forwards more quickly. Re-emphasise the 'fast feet and tiny steps' before each start. The race is not to see who moves forwards fastest, but rather who can get the most steps in over the specified distance.

Progression: Try a timed race – who can perform the most steps in 10 seconds?

drill 2 shuttles

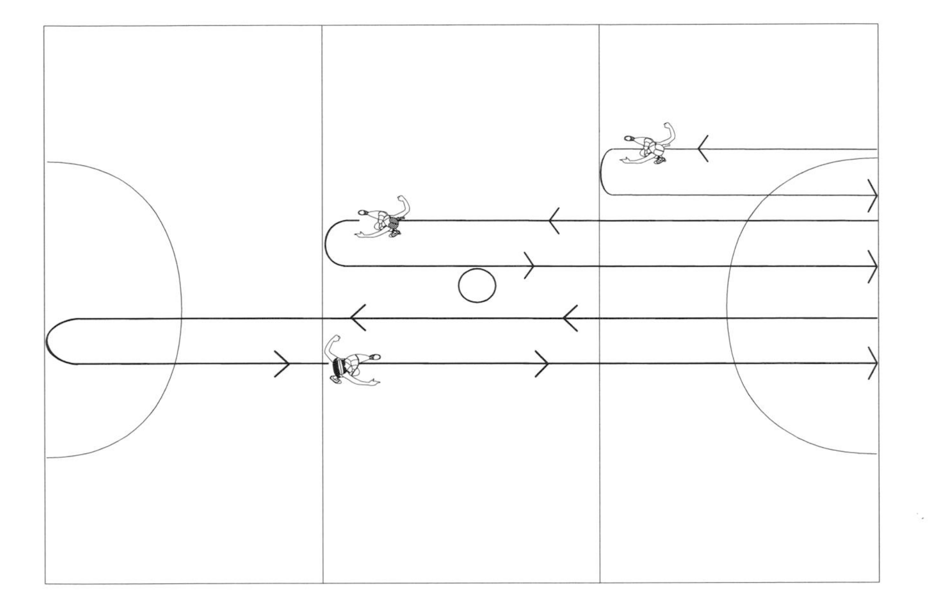

Objective: To warm up the body and practise pushing off on one foot to change direction and keep movement balanced.

Equipment: The whole length of the court.

Description: Players line up along the base line. On the coach's whistle, the players jog to the first third line, then turn to return to the base line by pushing off on their landing foot and turning their shoulders to transfer the balance of weight and change direction. The players then jog to the second third line and back, then to the other base line and back, each time performing the same action to turn.

Coaching points: Watch for a tendency to forget to change direction by pushing off on one foot and turning the shoulders, which reduces the player's balance.

Progressions: Jog to the line then sprint back, always keeping a balanced change of direction. Pair up the players and run shuttles in relay. Player 1 jogs or sprints to the third line and back, then player 2 repeats, and so on until the whole court has been covered.

drill 3 ball thief

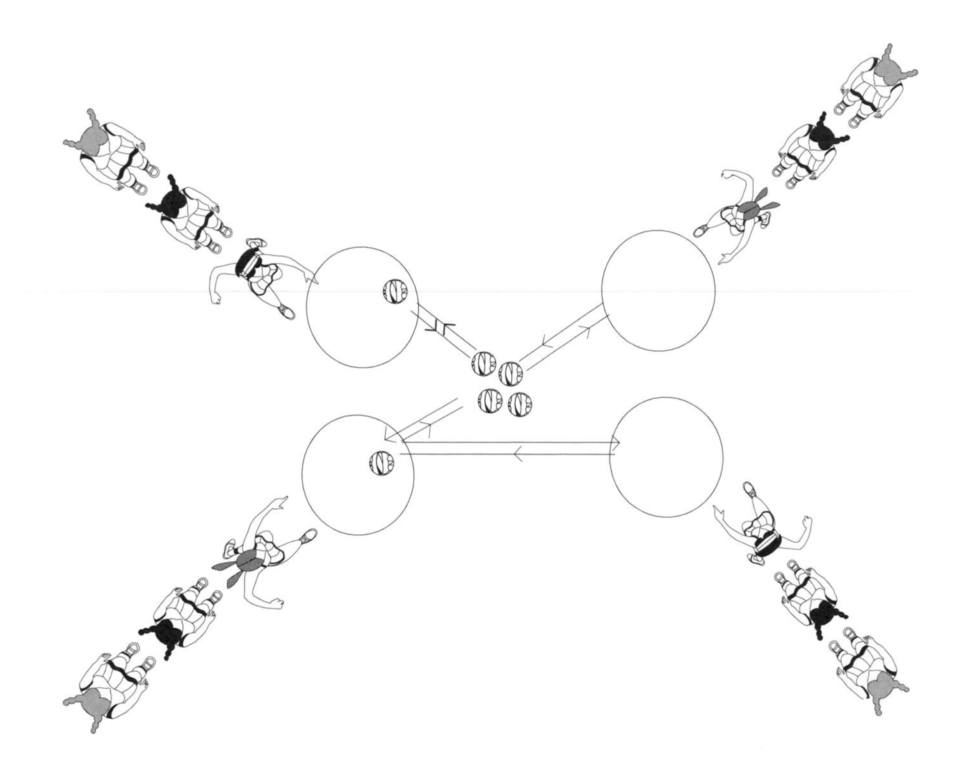

Objective: To develop communication skills and speed.

Equipment: Four hoops (or chalked circles) and six balls.

Description: At each corner of a square (about 5 m wide) place a hoop/circle – these will be 'home base' for each team. Divide the players into four teams and stand them in line, one team behind each base. Place eight balls in the centre of the square. On the coach's command, one player from each team runs to the centre to grab one (and only one) ball before returning to base to place it in their hoop/circle. Then the next player in line sets off to grab another ball. Once all the balls have gone from the centre the runners can steal a ball from the other bases. This continues until one team has three balls in their home hoop/circle. If no-one wins within a set time the coach can add another ball to make success a little easier.

Coaching points: Watch out for cheats picking up two balls at a time! Encourage each team to talk to their runner to make her aware of what else is going on around them.

drill 4 cats and dogs

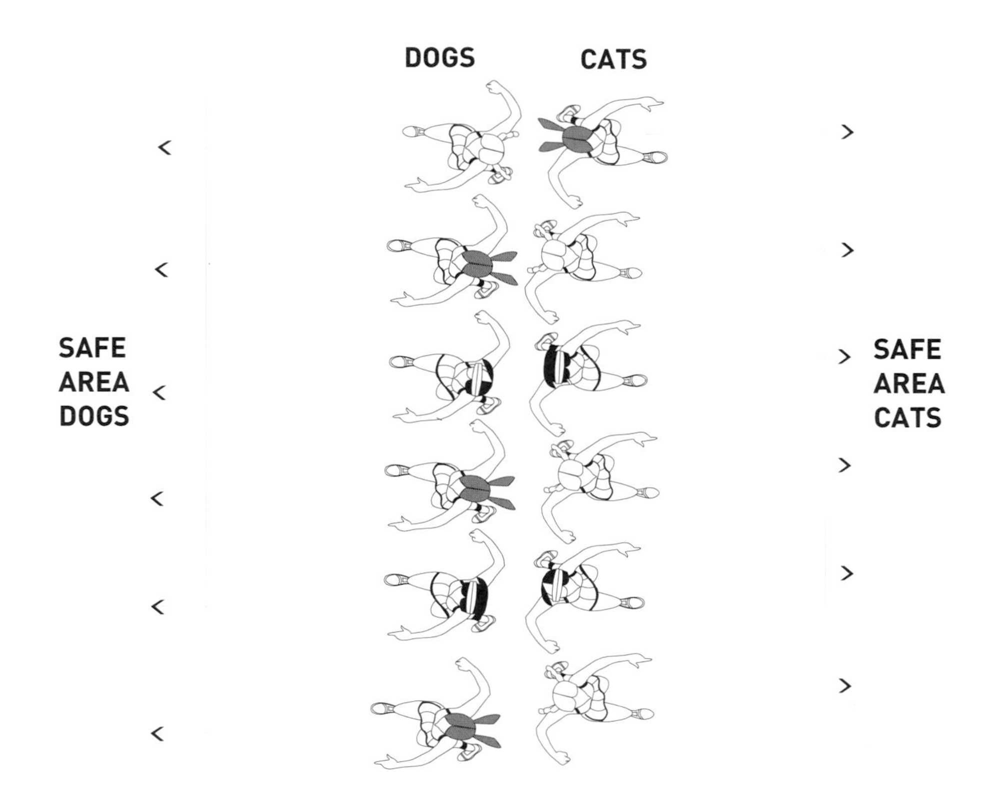

Objective: To warm up, practise quick movement and improve reaction to others.

Equipment: Players.

Description: Players line up in two lines back to back, with either everyone standing or everyone sitting. One line is called the 'Cats' and the other line the 'Dogs'. If 'Cats' is called out, those players have to run to a designated area, chased by their 'Dog' partner. If 'Dogs' is called out, the 'Dogs' run and the 'Cats' chase.

Coaching points: Look for balanced movement and quick responses.

Progression: Increasing or decreasing the working area will encourage more sprinting, dodging and so on.

drill 5 crazy groups

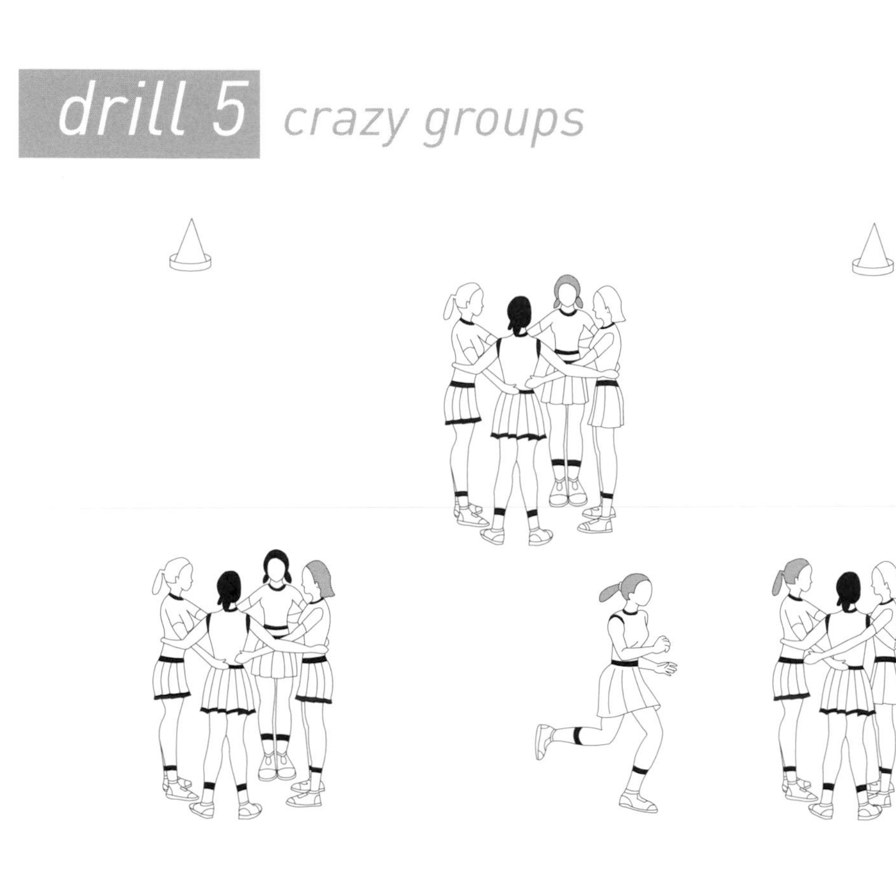

Objective: To warm up and encourage concentration.

Equipment: Players.

Description: On the coach's command the players must form groups as per the instruction. For example, if the coach calls 'Fours!' the players must form groups of four, all holding hands with each other and so on.

Coaching points: Once the players have grasped the principle of this drill it can be introduced unexpectedly (with a forfeit for the last group) into any part of the session, just to keep everyone on their toes. This is meant to be fun so don't make the forfeits too arduous!

Progression: Add four cones around the perimeter of the working area. Each cone is given a letter, A–D. On the coach's command all the players have to run around the designated cone before forming into their groups.

drill 6 dodge tag

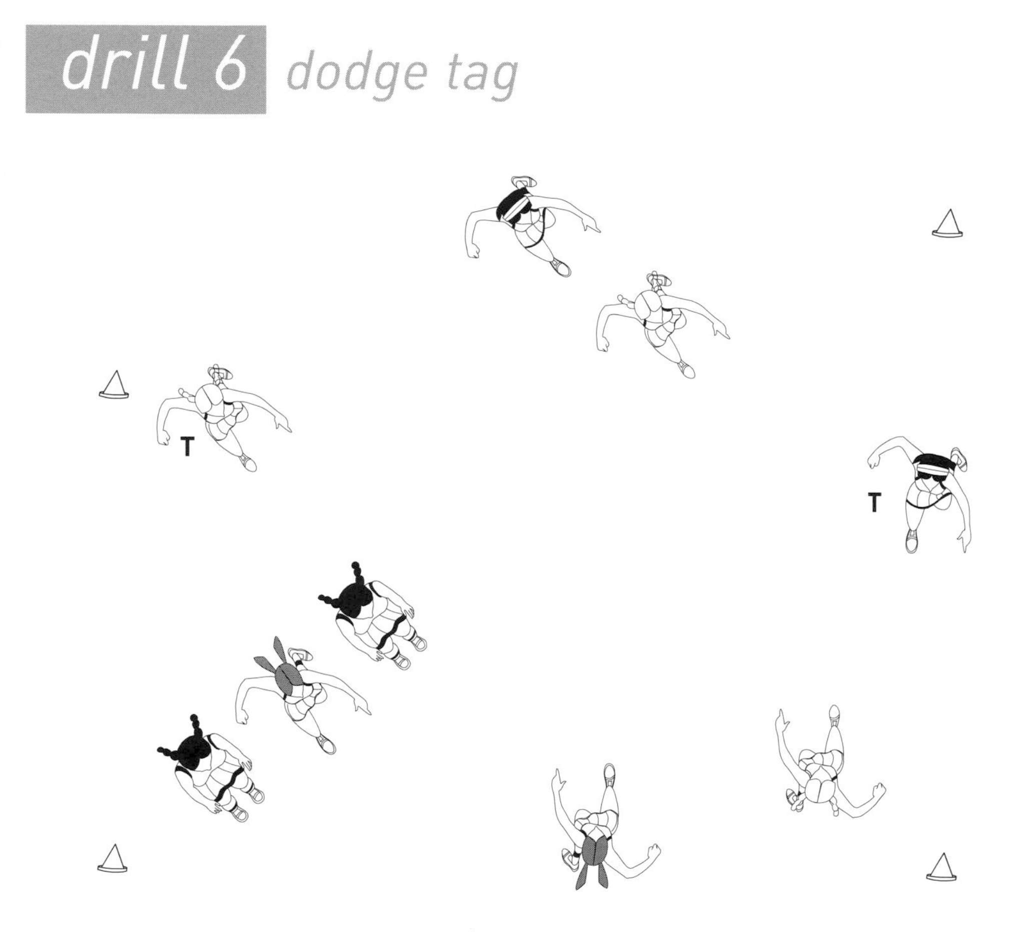

Objective: To practise dodging skills and improve balanced movement.

Equipment: Players.

Description: The playing area selected should be sufficient to allow players to run around but not so large that it allows full freedom of movement. One third of the court is ideal, or you can reduce the size of the working area using cones. Two players are taggers (T). The rest of the players must dodge out of their way and avoid being tagged. Players who have been tagged must stand still, creating barriers for the other players to dodge around.

Coaching points: Encourage players to make a definite dodge move to avoid the obstacles. Look for quick changes of direction, pushing off on the outside foot and using hips and shoulders to help keep balanced. All footwork should be balanced and controlled.

Progression: Reduce the size of the playing area and increase the number of taggers.

drill 7 high kicks

Objective: To develop strength and movement skills.

Equipment: Players.

Description: Starting on the side line, players march out to the centre of the court performing a series of high kicks, clapping their hands under the thigh with each stride. Each leg lift must be as high as possible and the drill must be kept under control. The objective is perfect form, not speed.

Coaching points: Insist on straight legs during this movement. Don't allow the body to curl towards the knee. It doesn't matter how high the straight leg comes as long as the form is perfect. Over a period of time the range of movement will improve and develop.

Progression: Give each player a marker (anything will do – margarine-tub lids are fine). Ask them to stomp out for eight strides, put the marker down and, after walking back to the start, try to reach their marker in fewer strides.

drill 8 high knees

Objective: To learn to lift the knees fast and high when running to aid stride length, reduce foot-to-ground contact time and therefore increase speed.

Equipment: Players.

Description: Split the players into four lines (A, B, C and D). A and B stand on one side line with lines C and D facing them on the other side line. Line A runs slowly forwards with knees pulled fast and high to the chest, keeping the thighs in line with the direction of running. When they reach the other side, line C begins the drill, then line B and so on. In this way each line has plenty of rest.

Coaching points: Insist on quality at all times. Allow lots of recovery time between sets. As players tire there will be a tendency for bodies to sag and knees to splay outwards. If this happens, stop the players and re-assert the aims of the drill. There is no need for fast-forward motion – foot speed is everything here.

Progression: With older players, encourage criticism and observation so they become their own coaches. Remember that form and quality are everything!

drill 9 hollow sprints

Objective: To develop a marked change of pace.

Equipment: Five cones.

Description: Divide the court into four 4 x 5 m areas using five cones. Starting at the first cone, players accelerate gently over the first 5 m to the second cone, run at full pace to the third cone, decelerate to three-quarter pace to cone four and hold until the last cone, then accelerate to full pace until the finish line. Walk back to the start slowly to recover.

Coaching points: Here the players are training their bodies to go fast, so they need to perform this drill while they are reasonably fresh. You must also allow plenty of rest between sets to ensure that every set is top quality. If you use this drill when players are tired they will never get the feeling of travelling fast. Tell the players to concentrate on how it feels. When they accelerate, they should drop the hands and lean slightly forwards. This will help to ensure that the power delivered by the legs is propelling the players forwards. Look for changes of speed at the marker points showing control of the pace.

drill 10 back to backs

Objective: To develop speed and endurance.

Equipment: Four cones.

Description: Mark out a run of 10 m, then 5 m, then 10 m. Players gently accelerate from the first to the second cone, then run flat out for 5 m. They then use the final 10 m to decelerate, turn around and start accelerating to the second cone to perform the drill again. There and back is one rep. Each player completes two reps and then walks slowly to fully recover before going again. Start with three sets of two reps and build up slowly over a period of weeks.

Coaching points: Encourage a real change of pace and controlled movement.

Progression: Use stopwatches to record times over the middle 5 m. Increase reps by one or two per session while ensuring the quality of the middle section is maintained.

drill 11 skipping race

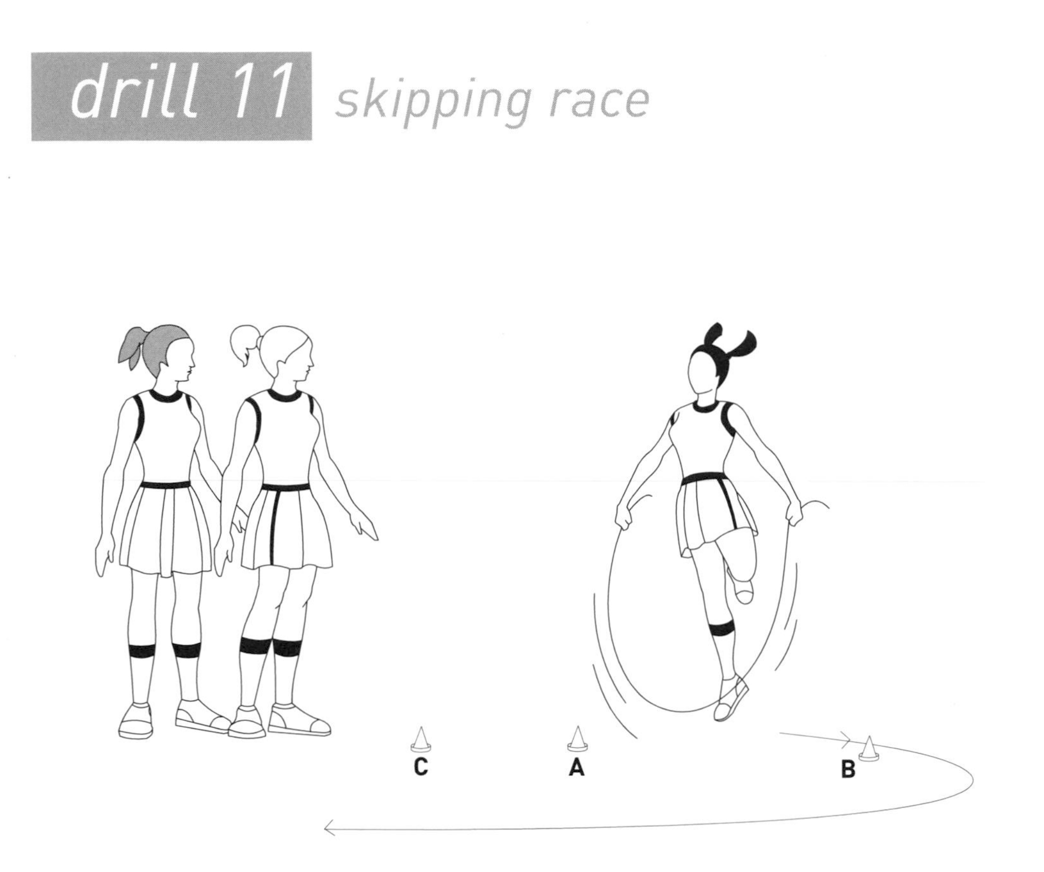

Objective: To warm up using plyometrics, reaction training and speed work.

Equipment: Two teams, six cones, two skipping ropes.

Description: Set up the cones as in the illustration above. Teams line up one behind another. On the command the first player in each team runs to cone A, picks up the rope and skips on the spot. On the second command the rope is dropped (not thrown) and the player runs backwards to cone B, around it and sprints home to high-five the next player at cone C, who then begins the drill.

Coaching points: Players running backwards should drive hard but stay under control. A key element here is the change from backwards to forwards running; the weight should be propelled forwards by pushing off on one foot.

Progressions: Introduce a ball. At cone B the player stops, receives and returns a pass from the next person in their team and then races back to the start. The receiving player at C puts the ball on the floor for the next player to pick up. Introduce different steps to add variety.

 drill 12 the wall

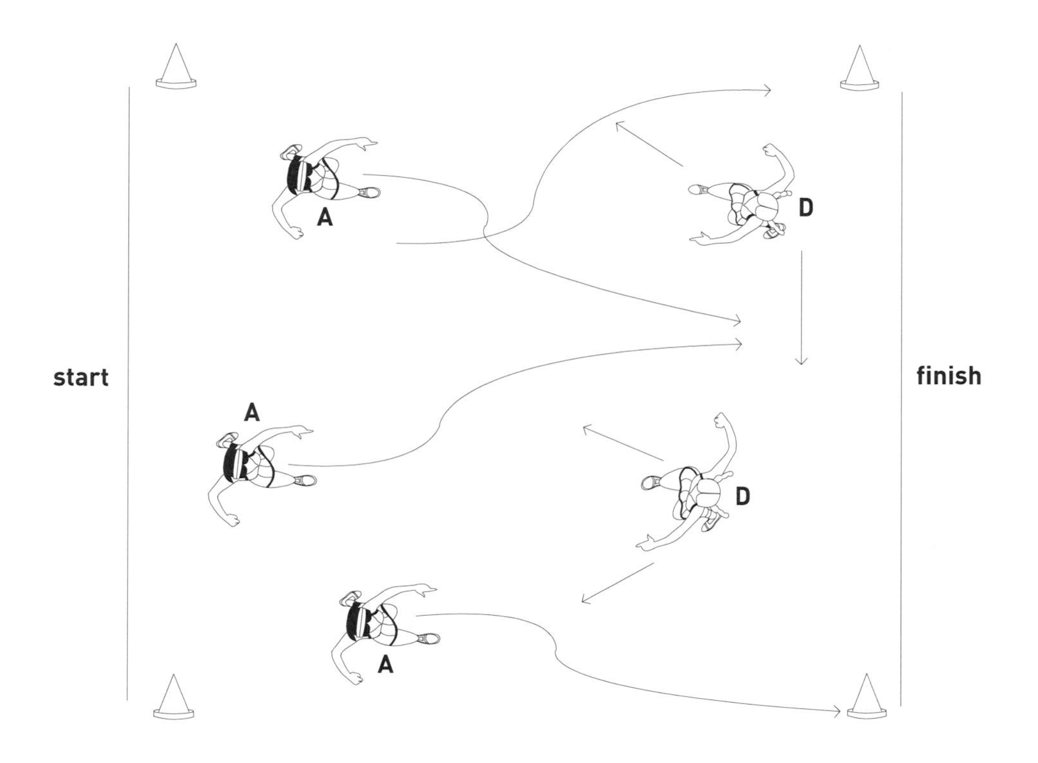

Objective: To warm up by running, dodging and reacting to other players.

Equipment: Four cones.

Description: Two or three defenders (D) stand in the middle of the playing area, the size of which should reflect the age and number of players. On the coach's whistle the other players (attackers or A) try to cross the 'wall' of defenders to reach the other side of the playing area without being tagged. If a player is tagged she joins the defending wall.

Coaching points: Keep the grid small to encourage dodging and sprinting. Ensure players tag below shoulder height for safety.

Progression: Change the footwork patterns of the defending wall and running players. For example, they can run using side steps, and dodge using a push off one foot to change direction.

drill 13 reaction drill 1

Objective: To practise quick reactions to develop hand–eye co-ordination.

Equipment: One ball between two players.

Description: Player A is working with player B feeding the ball. Player A stands opposite player B, approximately 1 m apart. Player A lightly places her hands on her head. Player B drops the ball from different heights in front of player A, who tries to catch the ball before it hits the ground. The players take it in turns to catch the ball.

Coaching points: Quick reaction time is the key so players need to concentrate.

drill 14 reaction drill 2

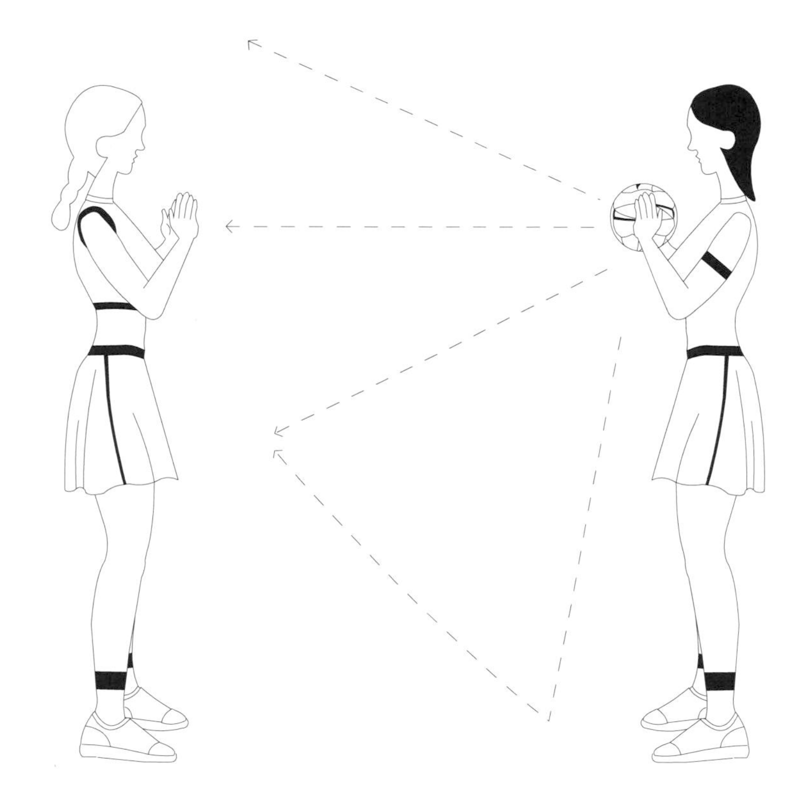

Objective: To encourage good reactions.

Equipment: One ball between two players.

Description: Players face each other approximately 2 m apart. The defender (D) runs quickly on the spot using small steps. The attacker (A) passes or drops the ball in any direction within arm's reach of D. D catches the ball and returns it to A.

Coaching points: All passes should be quick and catch the defender off guard. The defender should aim to stay balanced and in control of her movement and passes. Ensure quality at all times and do not allow wayward passes.

Progression: Forfeits can be included for wayward passes from either person or if the defender stops running.

drill 15 side jumps

Objective: To improve general agility; to condition the groin muscles (adductors and abductors); to prevent imbalance injuries and stabilise the prime muscle groups.

Equipment: The width of the court.

Description: Split the group into four lines (A, B, C and D), A and B on one side line and C and D on the other. All players face up the court so they are side on to each other. With good posture, line A side-jumps across the court aiming for height and distance on each jump. Line C then begins the drill, and so on.

Coaching points: Insist on quality at all times. Allow lots of recovery between sets. As players tire there will be a tendency for bodies to sag and for players to twist into a run. Looking backwards to where they came from will help players keep their bodies in the correct position. There is no need for fast forward movements – height and 'hang time' are what you want to see.

Progression: With older players encourage criticism and observation so they become their own coaches. Remind them that form and quality are everything!

drill 16 high skipping

Objective: To condition the hip flexors, extensors and calf muscles; to teach forceful and short ground contact time in order to develop speed.

Equipment: The width of the court.

Description: Split the group into four lines (A, B, C and D), A and B on one side line and C and D on the other. With good posture, line A high-skips across the court. When they reach the other side line, line C begins the drill and so on.

Coaching points: Insist on quality at all times. Allow lots of recovery between sets. Teach good, tall posture, with the top of the head held high. The players should aim for the greatest possible height and knee lift, with the front leg raised so that the soles of the shoes are visible to observers in front. Use the arms to assist the lift.

Progression: With older players encourage criticism and observation so they become their own coaches. Remind them that form and quality are everything!

drill 17 team passing v team running

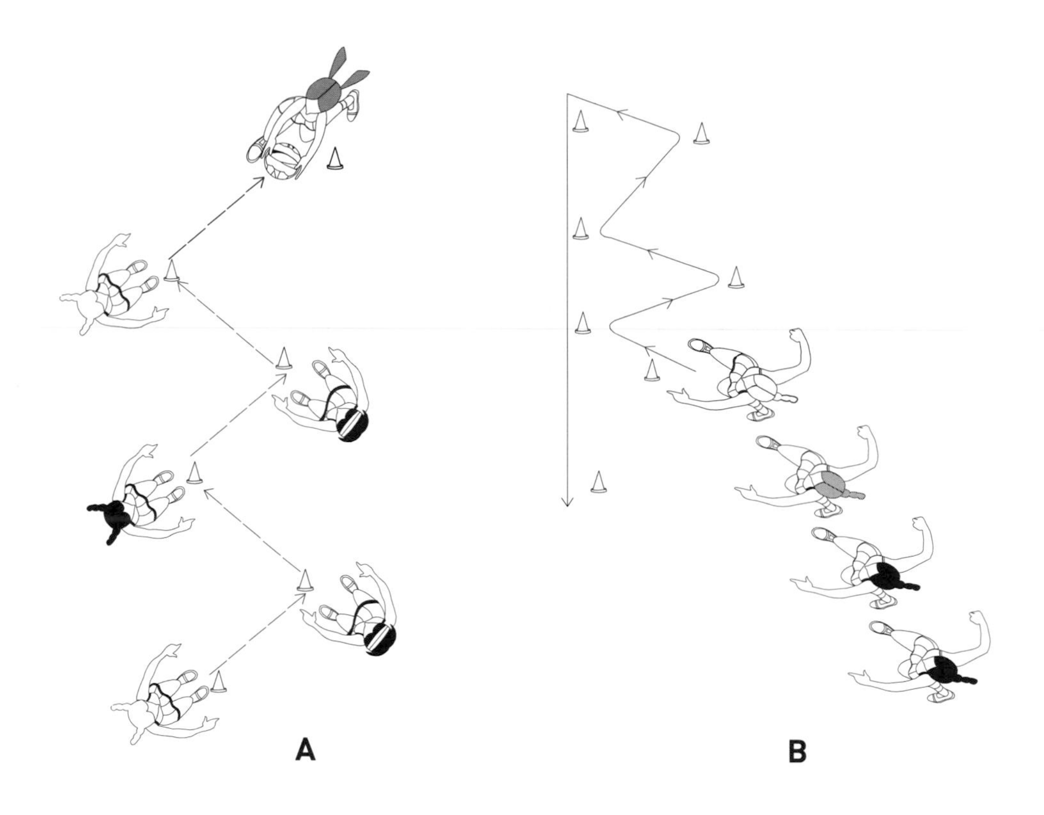

Objective: To warm up the body.

Equipment: One ball, cones.

Description: Players are divided into two teams. One team (A) spreads out in a zigzag formation about 3 m apart using half a court. This team passes the ball continuously up and down the zigzag. At the same time, the other team (B) runs in a zigzag over an area covering approximately two-thirds of a court, running one at a time in relay fashion. The passing team counts the number of passes completed in the time it takes all the runners to complete the course. Any pass dropped is not to be added to the total. The teams then reverse roles and compare scores.

Coaching points: Look for accurate, balanced passing. For the runners, movement should be balanced and controlled using quick steps and pushing off on the outside foot.

Progression: Vary the type of pass used. Vary the footwork pattern used.

drill 18 snakes

Objective: To warm up and have fun!

Equipment: One ball per team.

Description: Divide the group into teams with a maximum of six players per team. Each team lines up with the players one behind the other, 1 m apart with legs apart. Player A is the first player in the line and has the ball. On the coach's command, A rolls the ball through the legs of the other players in her line, then races to take up position at the back of the line and catch her own roll. Facing forwards, she picks up the ball and twists her upper body to pass the ball to the player in front, who takes the ball in both hands and twists the opposite way to give the ball to the next player. This left/right twisting motion is repeated until the ball is with the player at the front of the line, who starts the drill again by rolling the ball through the tunnel of legs once more. Repeat until all players have rolled.

Coaching points: While this is a 'young' drill, the twisting motion is a great warm-up for the upper body and with two teams racing each other it can be a lot of fun.

drill 19 zigzag shuttles

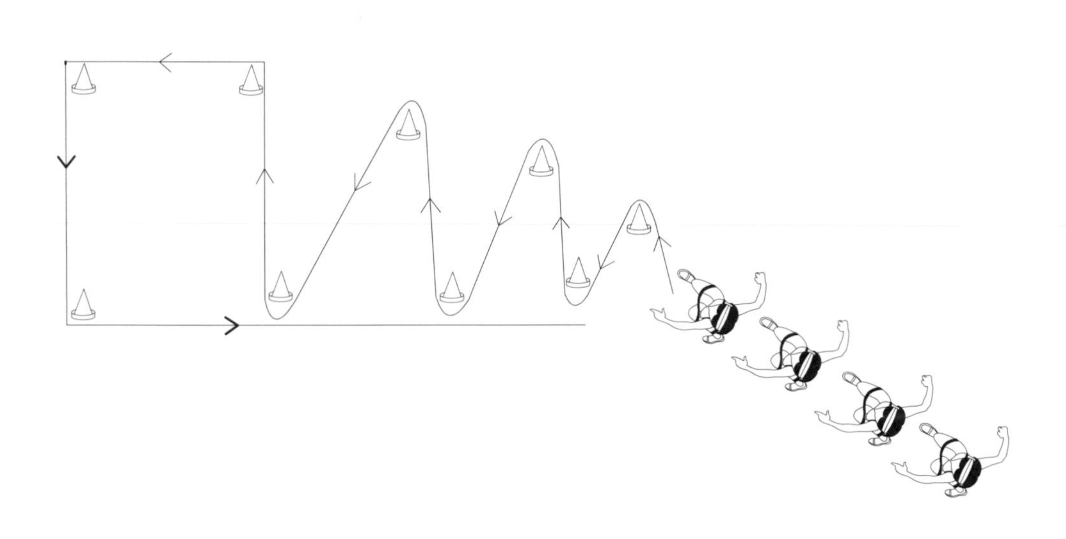

Objective: To warm up by practising sprinting and changing direction.

Equipment: Nine cones.

Description: Set out the cones as shown above over a third of the court. Players line up off court behind the first cone. On the coach's command, the first player jogs to the second cone, turns and sprints to the third cone, turns and jogs to the fourth cone and so on through the grid. When she reaches cone 8, she turns and jogs out to cone 9 then walks slowly back to the end of the line and waits her turn to go again.

Coaching points: Let the first runner get through two cones before the next runner sets off. Do not set the cones too far apart as a player will rarely sprint more than about 5 m on court, so anything longer than that in training is not beneficial. Keep the groups large enough that each runner has a good long recovery, but small enough that they do not get cold.

drill 20 horse and jockey

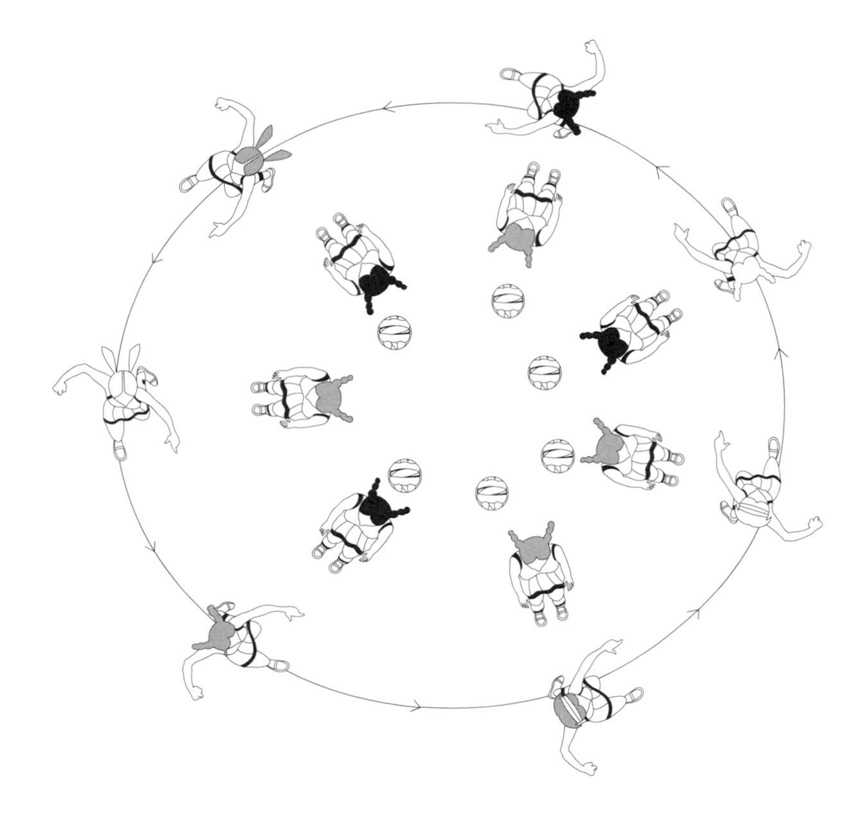

Objective: To warm up the body.

Equipment: Several balls.

Description: Arrange the players into two circles, one inside the other. A number of balls are placed in the middle of the inner circle. On the call of 'left' or 'right' the players in the outside circle have to run in that direction around the entire circle. Once the players get back to their starting positions they must go through the legs of a player in the inner circle and grab a ball. Players need to be on their feet before going for a ball.

Coaching points: Ensure plenty of rest between goes. This will ensure that the players practise high-quality speed and agility over a short distance.

Progression: The number of balls can be varied. For example, to increase the competition you can reduce the number of balls so only the quickest players get a ball.

New Zealand's Anna Rowberry demonstrates good chest-pass technique, with the ball held at chest height and the fingers spread wide behind the ball.

BALL SKILLS – PASSING AND CATCHING

It is fairly obvious that the ability to give and receive a pass is at the heart of the skills needed to become a good netballer. However, beyond the basics there are several elements within this training topic that can help develop confidence in throwing and catching the ball.

A common issue with younger, inexperienced players is that they consider possession of the ball to be the end in itself, rather than a link in a team chain. Many of the following drills that focus on passing and catching are also designed to give context to a pass – when, where and why we pass as well as how.

It is important to emphasise that the safe arrival of the ball is the responsibility of the passer – the aim of a pass is to transfer the ball to a co-player, not just to unload responsibility for it. It is the responsibility of the receiver to provide space and a target for the passer by indicating where they want to receive the ball by signalling with their hands.

As skills develop and drills require more movement, balance will become more and more important. Therefore, good practice is vital even within the more simple drills – check–receive–pass–move – maintaining control and balance at all times.

Once again there is the issue of when to stop and restart a drill. There is the constant danger of the players becoming embroiled in the fun of the drill (which is good) and losing sight of the skill that they are practising. It lies with the coach to spot when the drill is drifting and at that point he or she should stop the players and re-communicate the skill being practised and the objectives of the drill.

drill 21 ball tag

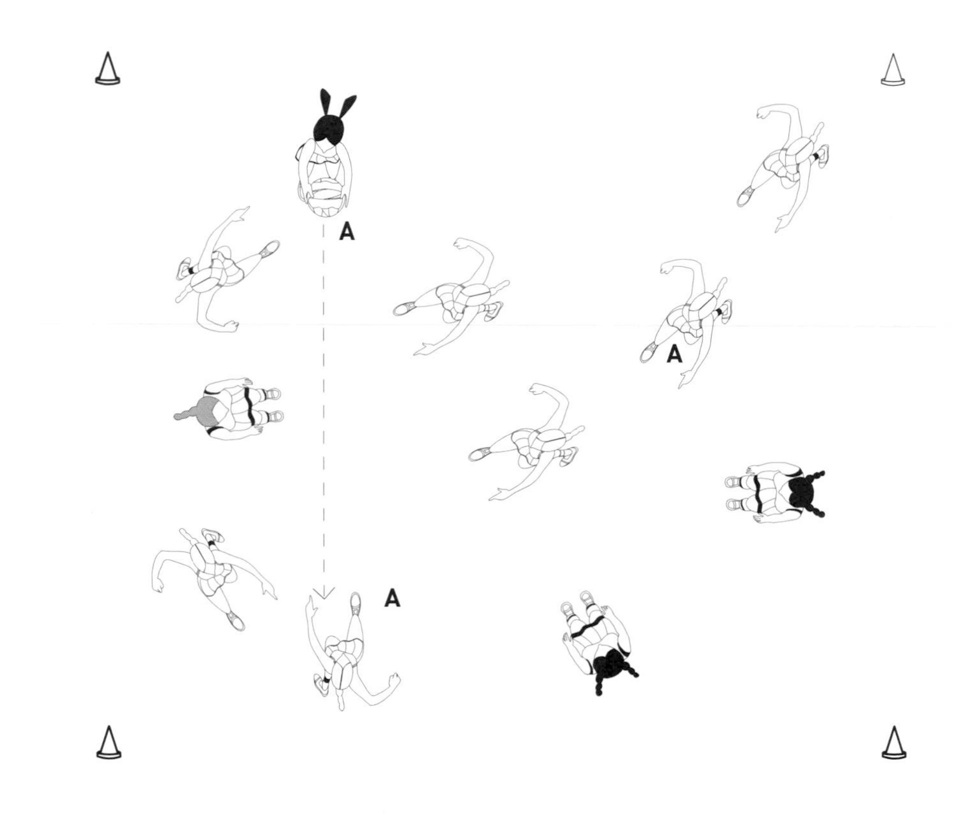

Objective: To develop communication and passing skills.

Equipment: One ball, four cones

Description: Use the cones to mark out an area equivalent to approximately one third of the court. There are three attackers (A) and lots of evaders. The aim is for the attackers to tag the evaders with the ball. Once tagged the evader must stand still. The attackers cannot run if they are in possession of the ball but can pivot on one foot.

Coaching points: Encourage lots of communication and movement between attackers. Look for quick but accurate passing.

Progression: Change the attackers regularly and see how many evaders they can tag in a fixed amount of time, for example two minutes.

drill 22 blind man's bounce

Objective: To improve reactions and develop movement skills.

Equipment: One ball and three hoops or chalked circles between two.

Description: Partners stand one behind the other, both facing the same direction. The hoops are set out in front of the players about a metre away at 10, 12 and 2 o'clock. The player behind has the ball. Without warning, she lobs it over her partner's head attempting to bounce it in one of the hoops. The thrower gets one point if she lands the ball in a hoop and the catcher gets five points if she catches it before it lands, two if she knocks it away before it lands and one if she catches it on the first bounce.

Coaching points: The thrower should use an underarm throw and ensure that the catcher is ready, hands up, on her toes, looking ready as well as being ready.

Progression: Move the target hoops further apart.

drill 23 piggy in the middle

Objective: To encourage good passing; to improve speed, anticipation and defensive marking skills.

Equipment: One ball between three players.

Description: Three players stand on any line on the court. The two end players are attackers (A) and the middle player is a defender (D).The attackers seek to pass to each other in any way they wish (bounce, chest, shoulder but not lobbed passes over the defender's head, as they are too easy). The defender scores a point for every interception. Attackers must keep one foot on the line. They can swap feet but must be in contact with the line when they pass and receive.

Coaching points: Encourage the defenders to be active by making themselves as big an obstacle as possible. Encourage them not to rely on reacting to a pass in order to block it but instead to be constantly moving and pressurising the attackers.

Progression: Use two defenders and increase the area in which the attackers work.

drill 24 the pivot

Objective: To practise changing direction by pivoting. Ideal for younger or inexperienced players.

Equipment: One ball between three players.

Description: The three players stand in a line approximately 2 m apart. Player A starts with the ball and passes it to player B. Player B receives the ball and pivots around to pass it to player C. The sequence is repeated in reverse.

Coaching points: Look for an accurate chest pass from all players. Player B should pivot keeping her landing foot in position and should only pass the ball once she is balanced and facing the direction in which she wants the ball to go.

Progression: Vary the type of pass used and speed up the passing.

drill 25 triangles

Objective: To develop quick, accurate passing and improve reaction time.

Equipment: Two balls between three players.

Description: Players A, B and C stand in a triangle sufficiently far apart to allow a chest pass between each player. Players B and C each have a ball. Player B throws the ball to player A who returns it. Player C then passes the ball to player A who returns it. This is repeated, seeing how fast the ball can be fed and received without anyone dropping it.

Coaching points: Quick, accurate passing and bags of concentration are essential.

Progression: Increase the distance between the players and change the type of pass to a shoulder pass or bounce pass, for example.

drill 26 catch-up squares

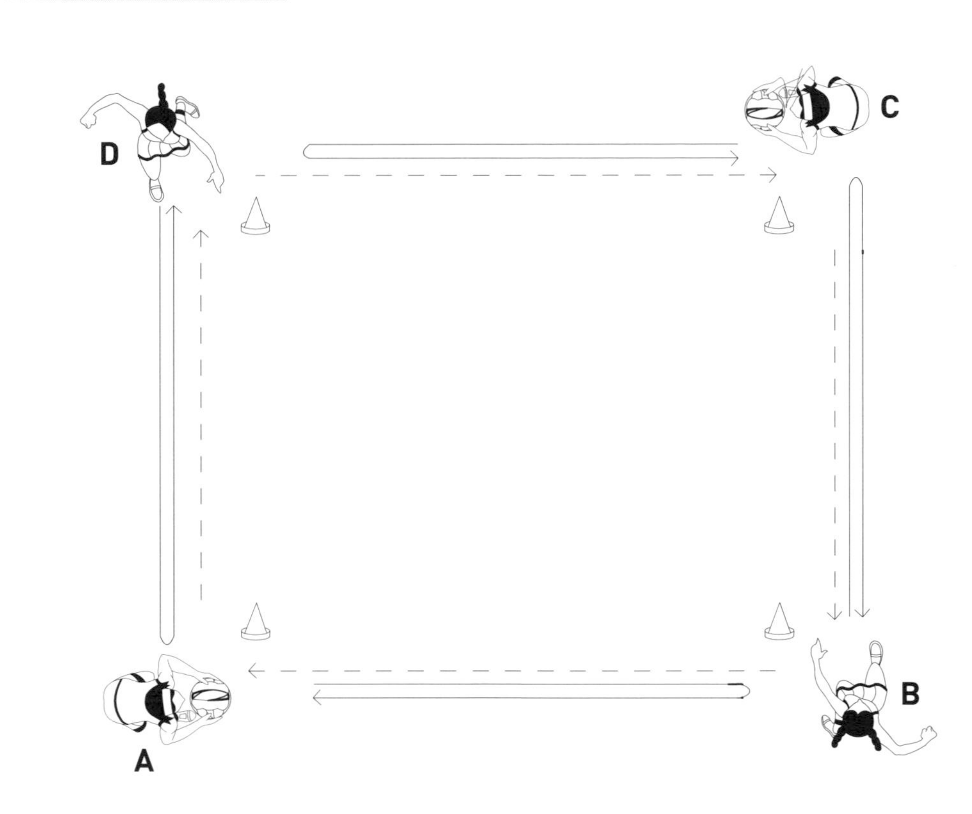

Objective: To improve passing and movement skills.

Equipment: Two balls and four cones.

Description: Set up a square with the cones about 3 m apart. The balls are diagonally opposite each other at the start. Players A and C roll a ball along the side of the square to the player at the 'free' corner (B and D). Players A and C then follow the ball by running to the next corner and back to receive the next 'pass'. A pass cannot be given until the receiver is back on station at their original corner. The objective is to catch up with the other ball or to last one minute – whichever comes first.

Coaching points: This drill will break down as soon as one ball catches up. At this point stop the drill and re-start from the beginning. Ensure that everyone concentrates on giving a good pass and not just 'unloading' in panic and appreciates that a ball travels faster than a runner – a good lesson in itself!

Progression: When the rolled ball version of this drill is mastered then move on to a bounce pass, chest pass and so on.

drill 27 passing relay

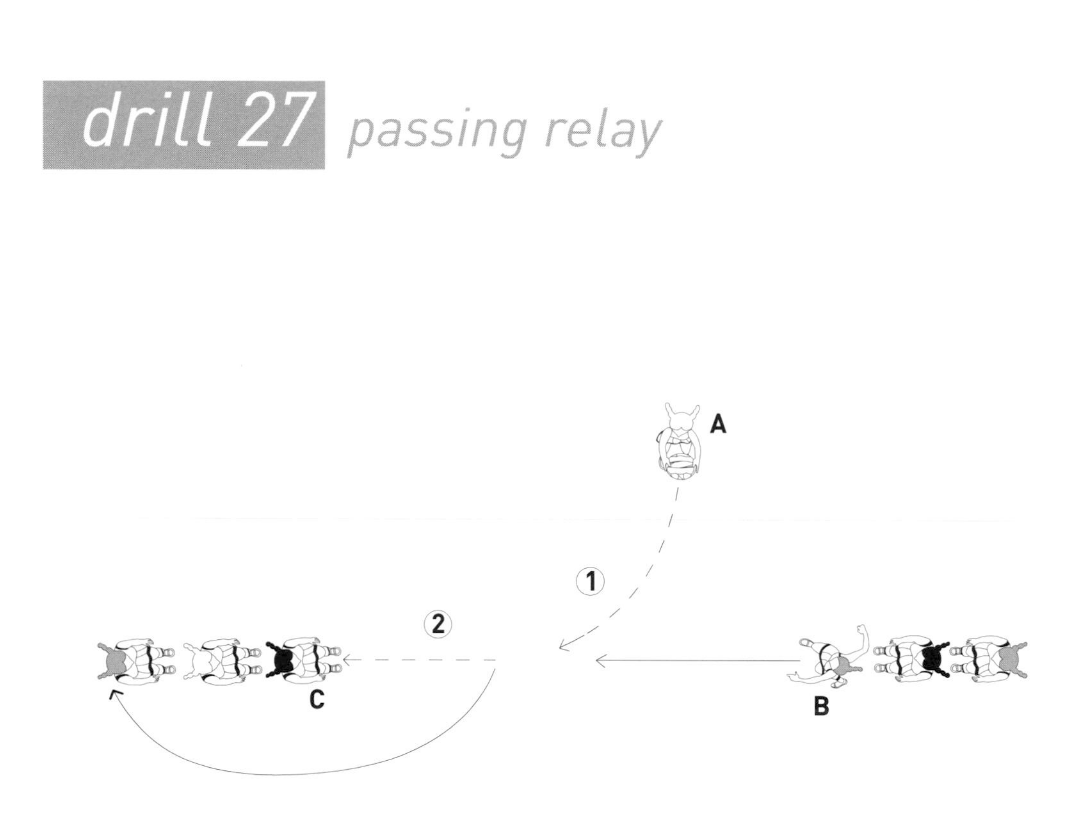

Objective: To practise running into a space to receive an accurate pass.

Equipment: One ball per group.

Description: Players form two lines facing each other approximately 8 m apart with player A, the feeder, standing with the ball halfway between the two teams. Player B runs towards the opposite team to receive a pass from player A. Player B catches the ball and then throws it to player C at the front of the opposite team. Player B then runs to the back of this line. Player C returns the ball to player A, then makes her run towards the opposite team to receive the next pass from player A, and so on.

Coaching points: Look for accurate passing with the ball passed into space in front of the receiving player. Players sprint to receive the ball, jumping with a balanced landing to avoid stepping before making a pass.

Progression: Rather than landing, stopping and passing, the ball should be released straight away. This running pass should still be balanced and accurate.

drill 28 circle drill

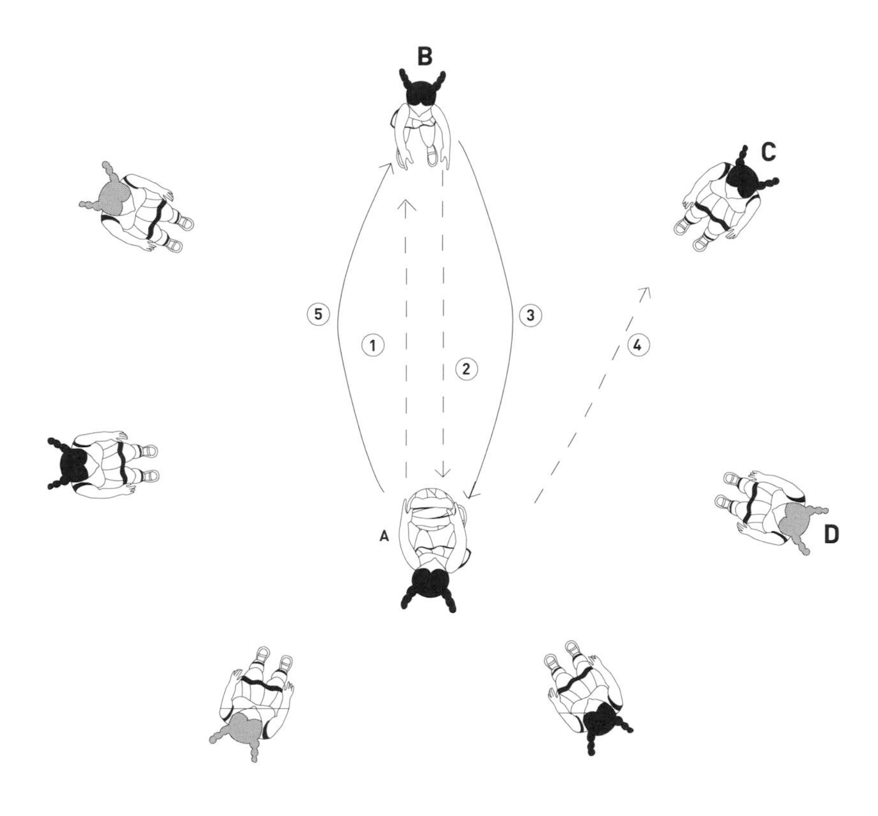

Objective: To practise passing and moving into a space.

Equipment: One ball, a chalked circle 5 m diameter.

Description: Player A stands in the middle of the circle holding the ball. She throws the ball to player B, who returns the pass to player A and follows the ball to the centre of the circle. Player A throws the ball to player C and moves out of the centre to the space in the circle left by player B. Player C passes the ball to player B in the centre, following the ball. Player B passes the ball to player D and moves into the space left by Player C, and so on.

Coaching points: Communication is vital – you can never have too much! The next receiver needs to be the eyes of the passer, who will have enough on her plate trying to avoid running players, catching and so on. The receiver needs to be in a position to take an easy pass.

Progression: The speed and type of pass can be varied. The player moving out of the centre can defend the ball as she moves out to the circle edge.

drill 29 passing square

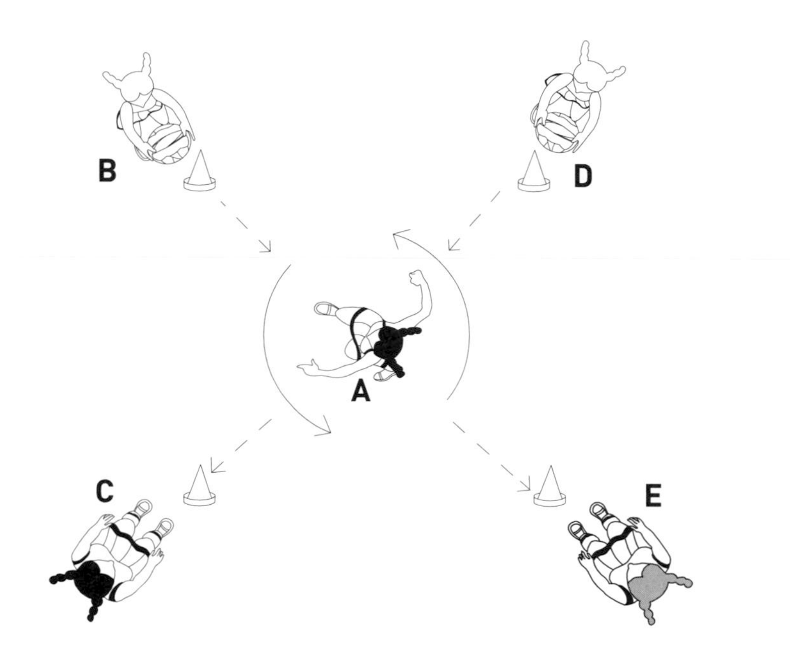

Objective: To practise passing and receiving the ball while changing direction by pivoting.

Equipment: Two balls and four cones between five players.

Description: Use the cones to mark out a square with sides of 3–4 metres, depending on the passing ability of the players. The distance between the cones should be large enough for the pass, but shouldn't place too much pressure on the players. Player A stands in the middle of the square with the other four players standing on the corners. Players B and D each have a ball. Player B feeds the ball to player A, who catches the ball and passes it to player E. Player A pivots to receive a pass from player D and passes the ball on to player C, and so on.

Coaching points: Ensure that one foot remains stationary while passing. Start the drill very slowly and only increase the pace once everyone has grasped it.

Progression: Vary the type of pass used and speed up the feed of the pass.

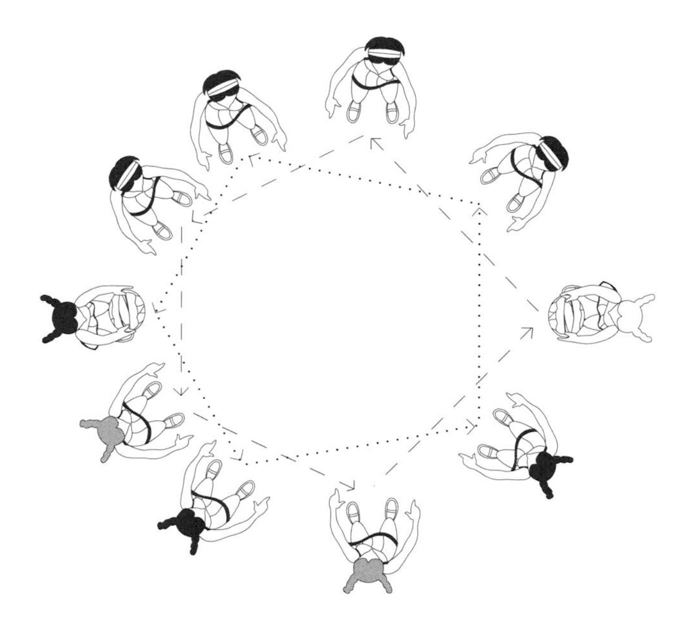

Objective: To practise catching and receiving passes while introducing an element of competition.

Equipment: Two teams with a minimum of four players in each, two balls.

Description: Two teams (A and B) stand in a large circle, each team taking alternate places. Players should stand at least one arm's width apart. Start with the balls on opposite sides of the circle, one with team A and one with team B. On the coach's whistle the ball is passed around the circle between members of the same team, i.e. players from team A pass their ball to each other only and players from team B pass the ball to each other only. The balls are passed in the same direction and the aim is to try and overtake the other team's ball.

Coaching points: The players will have to pivot to receive and give a pass.

Progression: As above, introducing a change of direction on the coach's whistle. Attempts at intercepting the opposite team's ball can also be introduced.

drill 31 receiving on the run

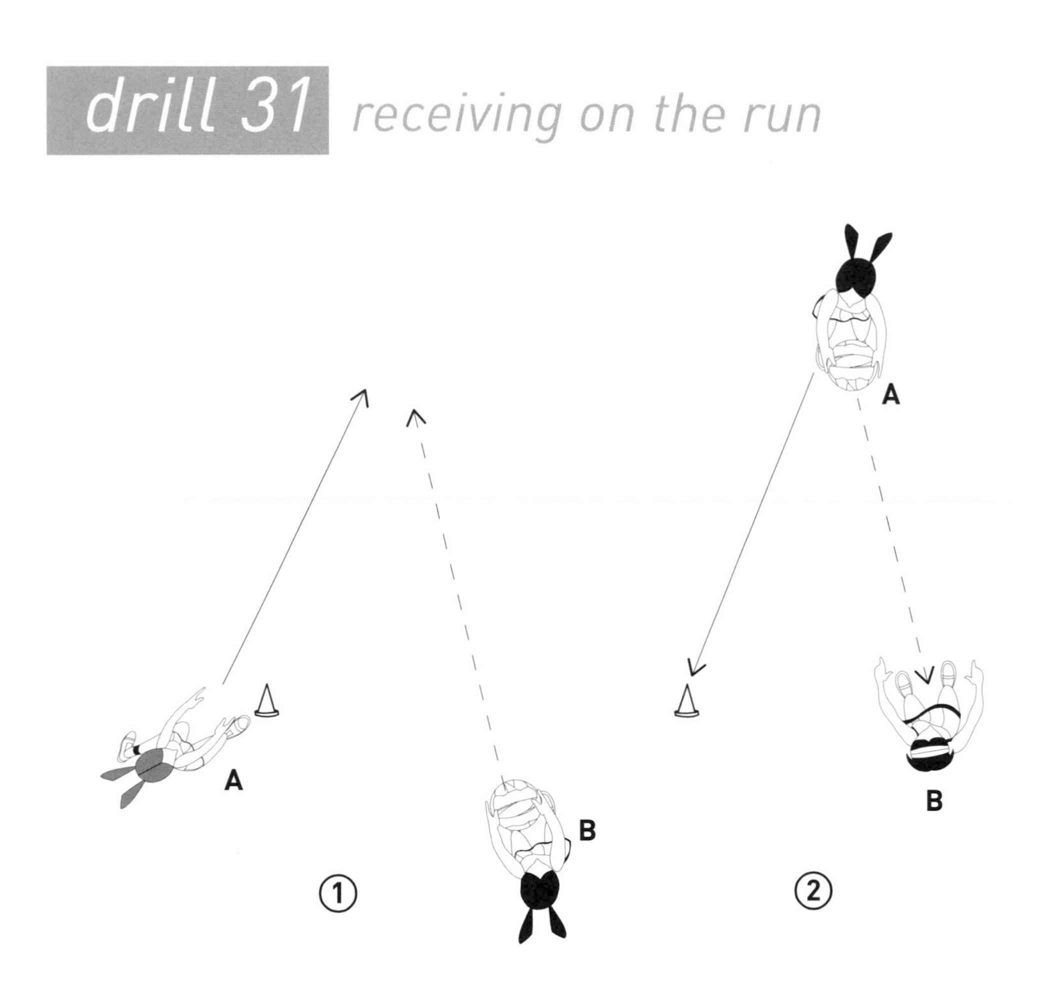

Objective: To develop spatial awareness and improve passing into space.

Equipment: One ball and one cone between two players.

Description: Partners stand facing each other approximately 2 m apart. A stands at the cone and on the coach's command runs diagonally to the right of player B, who passes the ball in front of the running player. A catches the ball, pivots and returns the ball to B. A returns to the cone. On the next command, A runs to the left and the pass into space is repeated. After five passes to each side, partners exchange roles. Repeat so each person runs and throws twice, then allow recovery. Discuss what has just happened and reaffirm drill objectives before re-starting.

Coaching points: Passes must be in front of the running player to ensure they run onto the ball and don't have to reach backwards or stop to catch the pass.

Progression: B calls 'left', 'right', 'front' or 'back' and A must respond by running in that direction to receive the pass.

drill 32 pea on a drum

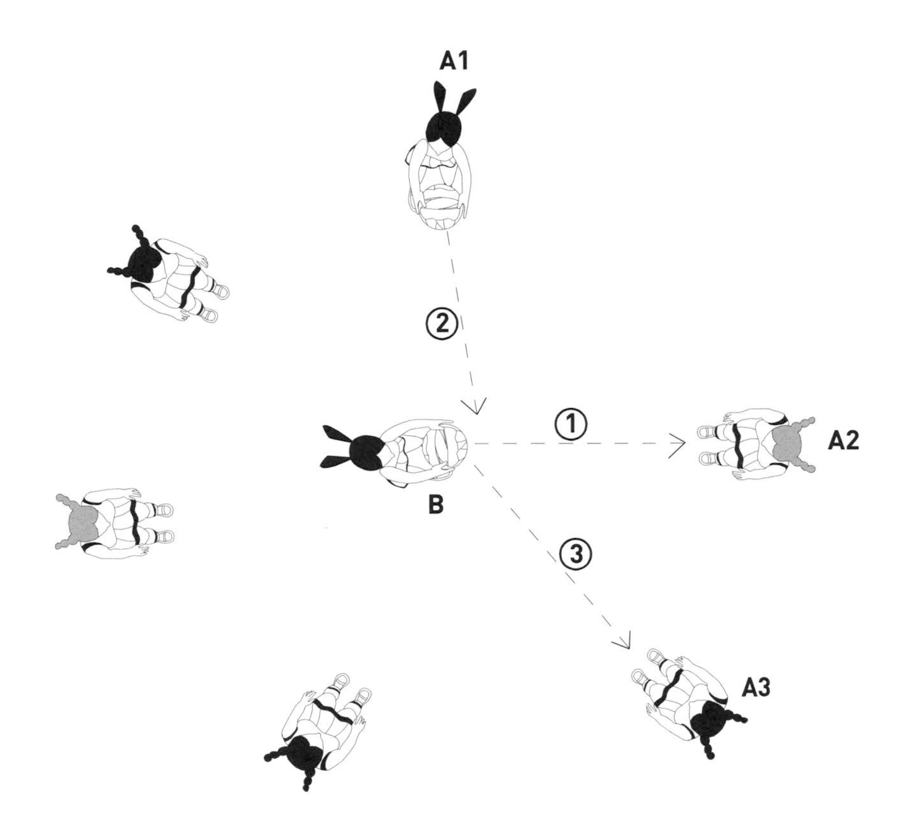

Objective: To practise passing under pressure.

Equipment: Two balls between at least seven players.

Description: Arrange six players (A1–A6) into a circle with the remaining player (B) in the centre with a ball. Another ball is given to A1. B passes the ball to A2. A1 then passes the ball to B who immediately passes to A3. The moment the pass is away A2 passes to B and so on. There is therefore a continuous stream of passes coming to B, who must receive and give quickly and accurately. Change player B regularly.

Coaching points: Don't sacrifice quality for speed. If the drill breaks down, return to slow, careful passing and then slowly build back up.

Progression: By increasing the spacing between the circle players, B will have to pivot to make the pass. Watch for footwork if you progress to this level. If you have a group that is really good at this (and perhaps getting a bit cocky) then call for changes of direction and type of pass.

drill 33 diamonds

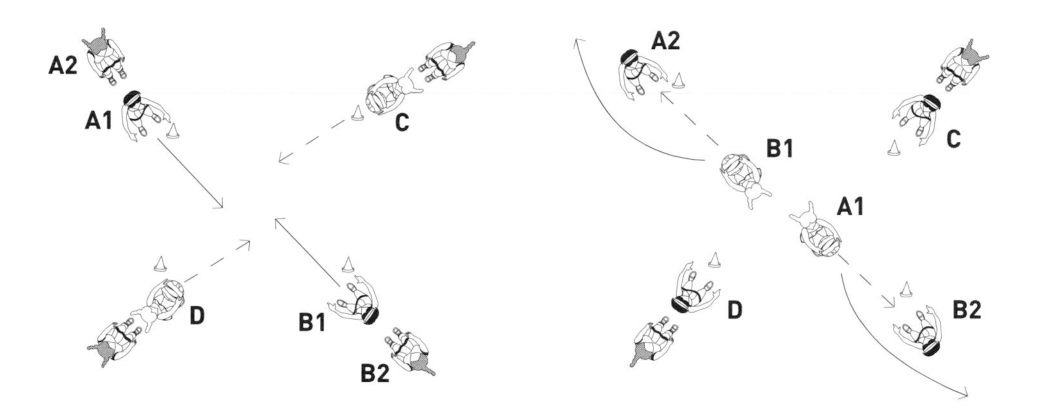

Objective: To improve movement skills, spatial awareness, communication and conditioning.

Equipment: Two balls and four cones between eight players.

Description: Place cones to form a square approximately five metres across. Two players stand at each cone. Players A and B are diagonally opposite each other, with players C and D at the other two cones with a ball. A and B run towards each other, and when they reach the middle of the square they each receive a pass from their left from C and D respectively. A passes forwards to the next player (B2) and B passes to player A2. A and B then run and stand behind the player to whom they passed the ball. C and D then run, receive the pass from A2 and B2 and so on.

Coaching points: Players should always receive the ball from the left and throw straight ahead. Walk through the drill a few times then build up speed gradually.

Progression: Perform the same drill but players receive passes from the right.

drill 34 passing clock 1

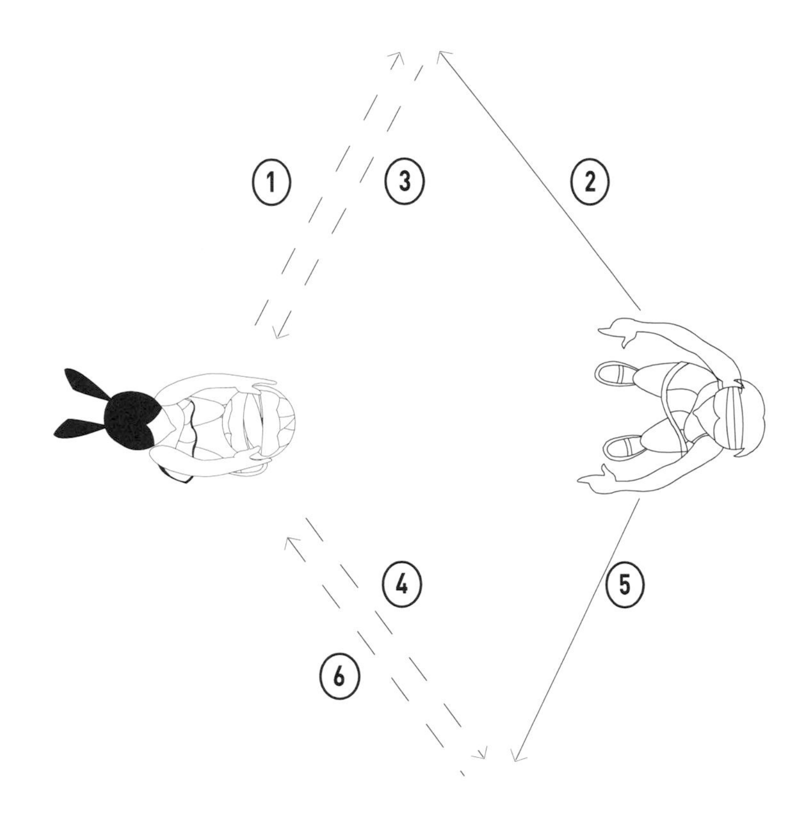

Objective: To develop co-ordination and condition the body.

Equipment: One ball between two players.

Description: Players 1 and 2 stand 2 m apart facing each other. Player 2 runs on the spot with fast feet. Player 1 makes a pass low to the left for player 2 to catch and return, then player 1 passes low-right, high-left, high-right and then finally over the head of player 2. Player 2 must turn quickly and receive the final pass before it hits the ground, pivot and make a chest pass back to player 1 to finish. Swap roles.

Coaching points: Ask for all the passes to come in rapid fire to put the catcher under some pressure. The final pass must be sensible and must give player 2 some chance of success.

drill 35 passing clock 2

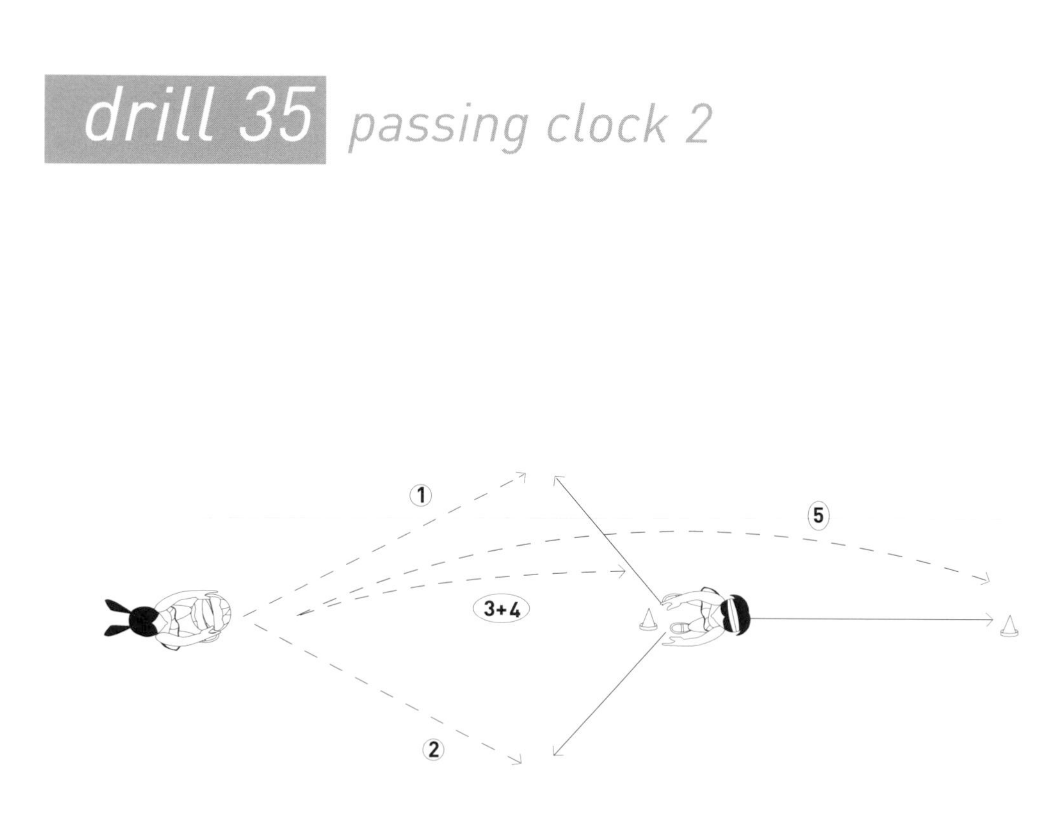

Objective: To develop co-ordination and condition the body.

Equipment: One ball and two cones between two players.

Description: Partners stand 2 m apart facing each other. Player 1 is at cone 1 with cone 2 about 5 m behind. On the coach's command player 1 passes to the left of player 2, who drives onto the ball to make the catch. Player 2 then backtracks quickly to the start position. Player 1 sends a pass to the right for player 2 to drive onto and return. Player 1 then gives two high passes that require player 2 to jump. Finally, player 2 turns to run to cone 2 to receive an overhead pass into the space. She then pivots and returns a flat chest pass. Swap roles.

Coaching points: Ask for all the passes to come in rapid fire to put the catcher under some pressure. The final pass must be sensible and must give player 2 some chance of success.

drill 36 flag drill

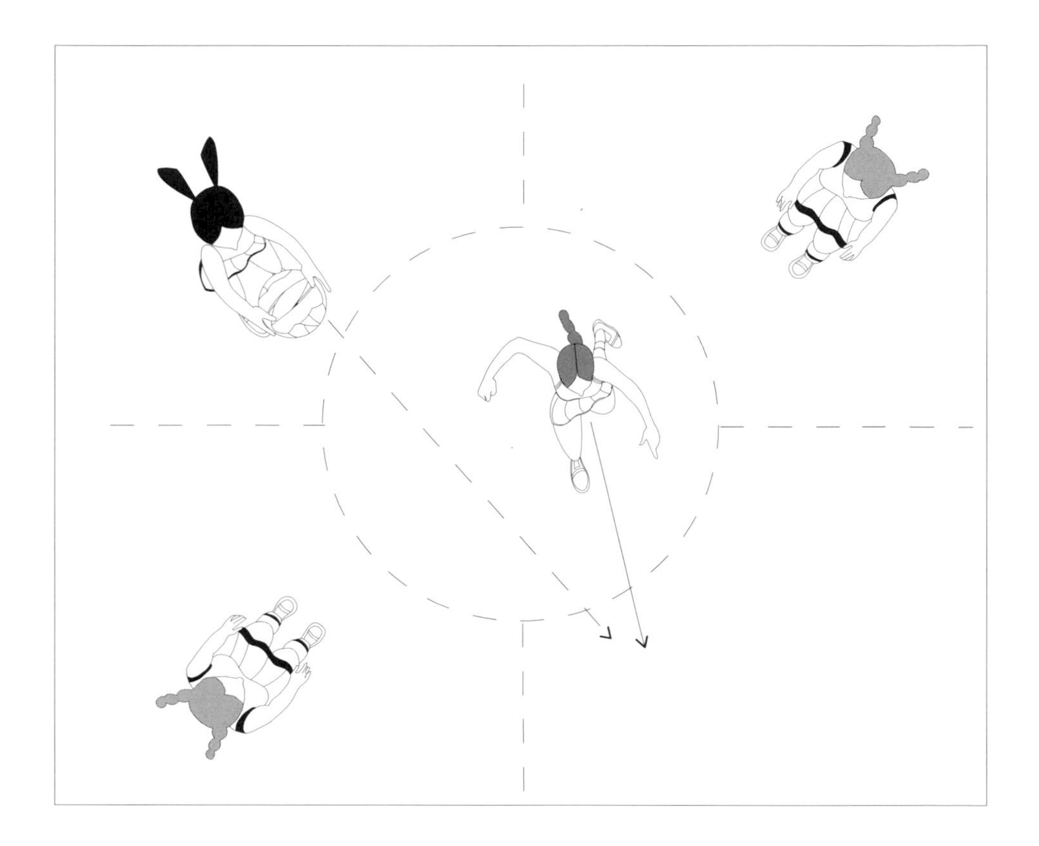

Objective: To practise using and creating space.

Equipment: Centre third of court divided into five spaces with cones, four players, one ball.

Description: The four players take up position as shown above, one per sector (there will always be one empty space). Player 1 has the ball. On the coach's command, player 1 passes to a player of her choice. Meanwhile the player closest to the empty space drives into it and calls for a pass. Players are asked to be aware of where the space is now and where it is going to be next.

Coaching points: Start off slowly so players can get a feel of the drill and only then speed things up. Never sacrifice quality for speed.

Progression: Build the drill by gradually adding one, two, three and then four defenders to the grid.

drill 37 passing confidence

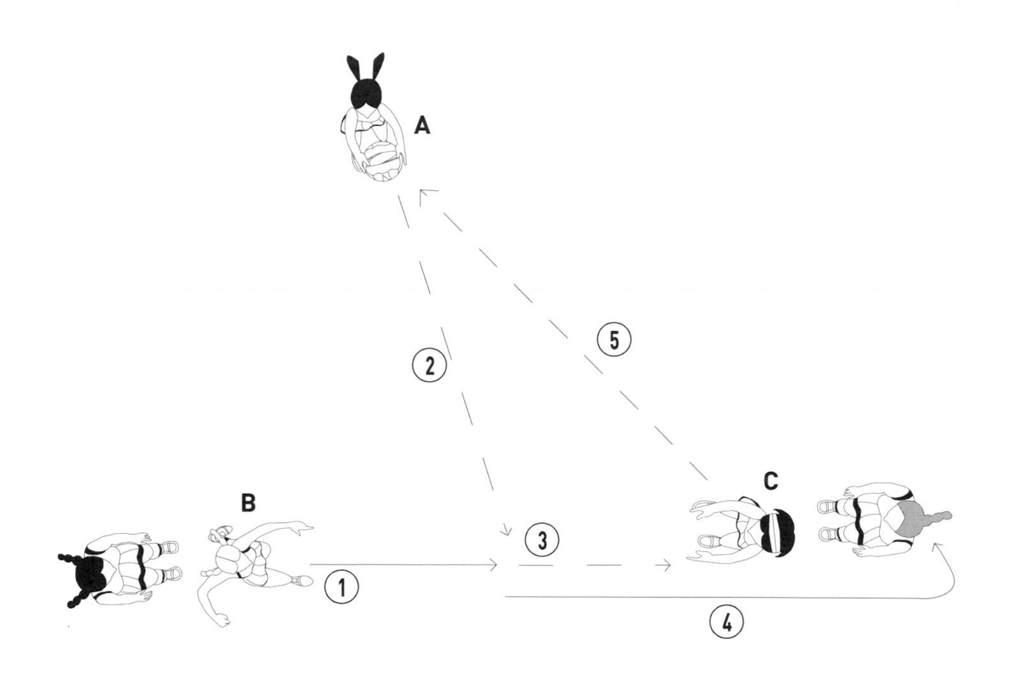

Objective: To develop passing confidence.

Equipment: One ball per group.

Description: Player A has the ball and is the feeder. Form the remaining players into two lines (B and C). Player B1 runs straight ahead onto a pass given by A to the centre point, catches the ball, chest passes to player C1 and runs to the rear of line C. Player C1 then passes the ball to player A, runs to take a return pass at the centre point, chest passes to player A2 and runs to the rear of line A, and so on.

Coaching points: The lines should have a maximum of four players each – any more than this and players will be standing around for too long. If you have a large group, form several drills. Make sure that player A passes into space for the runners to drive onto. In this way the players will get the feel of an active pass.

Progression: Place a cone in the centre and one at either side a metre away. The runner runs at an angle and dodges through the cone and back to receive the pass.

drill 38 driving grid

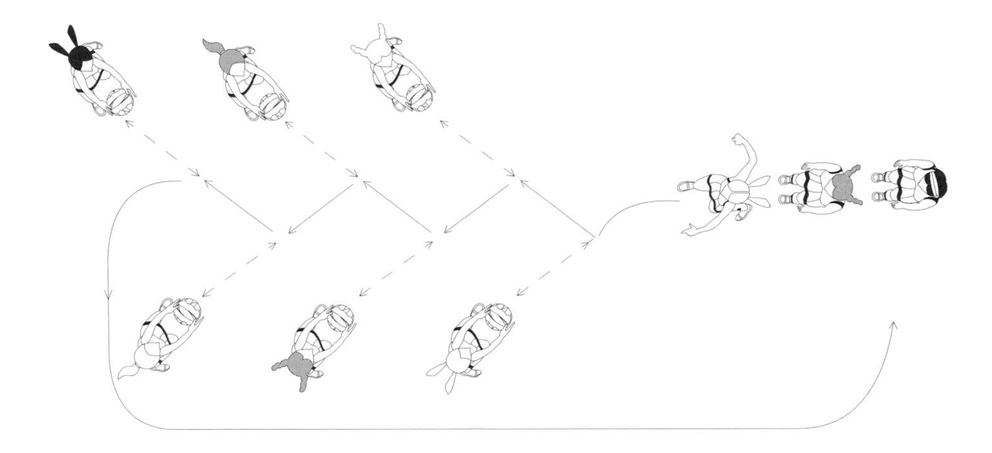

Objective: To develop catching confidence and condition the body.

Equipment: At least eight players with one ball between 2 players; five cones.

Description: Each passer (A) has a ball and is positioned in a large staggered grid as shown above. The remaining players (B) are the runners and form a line at the end of the area. Player B1 runs into the grid towards player A1, who passes the ball. With a two-footed landing, the ball is caught and then returned. Player B1 then pushes off quickly to head straight towards player A2, continues through the rest of the grid, then walks back to the start to recover. Player B2 now performs the drill.

Coaching points: Make sure that the Bs keep driving towards each ball strongly until it is caught. Stress the importance of balance and a good landing. Build the drill up slowly – it is designed to build confidence in receiving a strong pass on the move, but confidence must be built through success, not repeated failures!

Progression: Bring the As closer together, so the Bs have to change direction much more quickly. Change the type of pass.

drill 39 impossibility

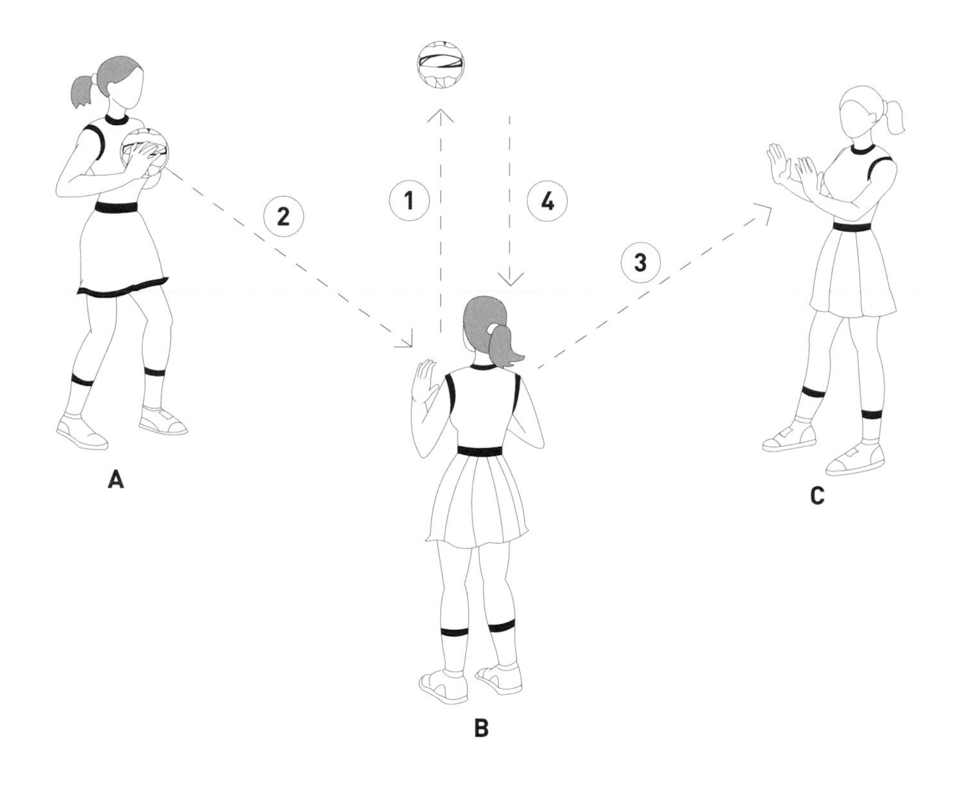

Objective: To improve passing under pressure – for experienced players.

Equipment: Two balls between ten players in a staggered line.

Description: A and B have a ball. B throws her ball up; at the moment the ball leaves her hands, A chest passes to B, who then passes to C, while her original ball is still in the air. The moment B recovers her original ball, she chest passes to C, who has in turn thrown her ball up to free her hands for her receive and return.

Coaching points: This drill requires a controlled vertical throw and bags of concentration. A must take the cue to pass from B's vertical throw and the pass must come in the moment the ball starts its upwards path. Introduce the drill in five-minute blocks each session to avoid players becoming frustrated.

Progression: Race two teams over a set distance, with A running to the end of the line after passing. Or try the drill in teams of four in a square so the pass is taken and given through 90 degrees.

Objective: To learn correct technique for the chest pass.

Equipment: One ball per pair.

Description: Starting with the players 3 m apart, have the players execute chest passes between each other.

Coaching points: This pass should be flat and firm, from chest height to chest height. Players should keep elbows high and fingers spread wide behind the ball and follow through to the target with the fingertips.

Progression: Once correct technique is understood, have the players widen the gap between each other to test where the limits of accuracy are.

drill 41 shoulder-pass practice

Objective: To learn correct technique for the shoulder pass.

Equipment: One ball per pair.

Description: Starting with the players 5 m apart, have the players execute shoulder passes between each other using alternating arms.

Coaching points: Players must master this pass from shoulder height on both sides and, as with the chest pass, should follow through to the target with the fingertips. Look for the body weight moving forwards to add power to the pass.

Progression: Once correct technique is understood, have the players widen the gap between each other to test where the limits of accuracy are.

MOVEMENT AND FOOTWORK

Footwork in netball is all about agility, change of speed and direction, control and balance. When practising footwork skills it is important to focus on the body's centre of balance and be in control of the body's momentum at all times.

Landing is an important skill to master. Jumping to catch the ball can help to control forward momentum and enable players to land without stepping. If you jump up to catch the ball, it is much safer to land on both feet. This also allows the player to choose their landing foot (around which they can pivot), giving more options for the next move.

Learning to land on one foot and then pivot gives players the opportunity to change the direction of the game, use open space and move the ball into different areas of the court. Landing on one foot also forms the basis of the running pass for experienced players, where the ball is released quickly while the player is still on the move. This can speed up the game and create attacking opportunities.

When working with younger players, coaches must remember that halting a moving body requires a considerable amount of strength. Keep drills that involve lots of changes of direction nice and brief so that quality remains high. There is no harm in rest!

drill 42 H drill

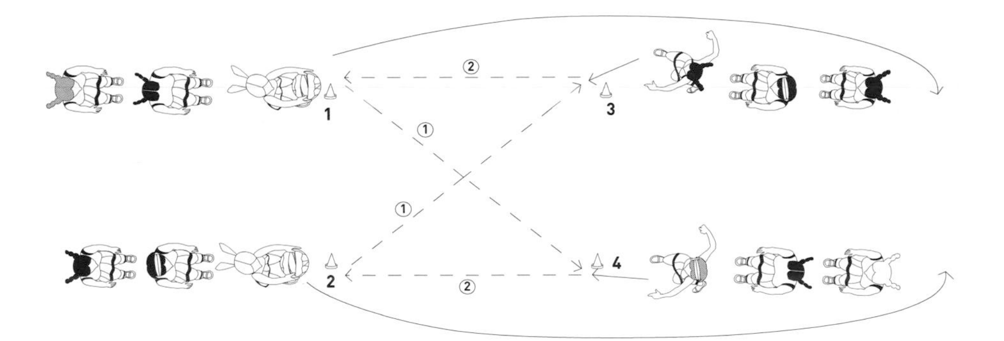

Objective: To practise passing into space, and to improve agility.

Equipment: Two balls, four cones.

Description: Using the centre third as the working area, divide the players into four teams and line them up behind the third lines as shown above. Place the cones approximately 1.5 m away from the third lines. The first players behind cones 1 and 2 shoulder pass diagonally into the space ahead of the first players behind cones 3 and 4. The passers then run to the back of the queue opposite them. The receiving players drive onto the pass and make a good landing before giving a straight chest pass to the next player in the queue opposite them, who drives onto the pass. The passers then run to the back of the queue opposite them, and so on.

Coaching points: Walk the drill through once so that everyone knows what they are doing. Encourage a good hard drive onto the passes.

Progression: Change the chest pass to a shoulder or a bounce pass.

drill 43 round the world/wink murder

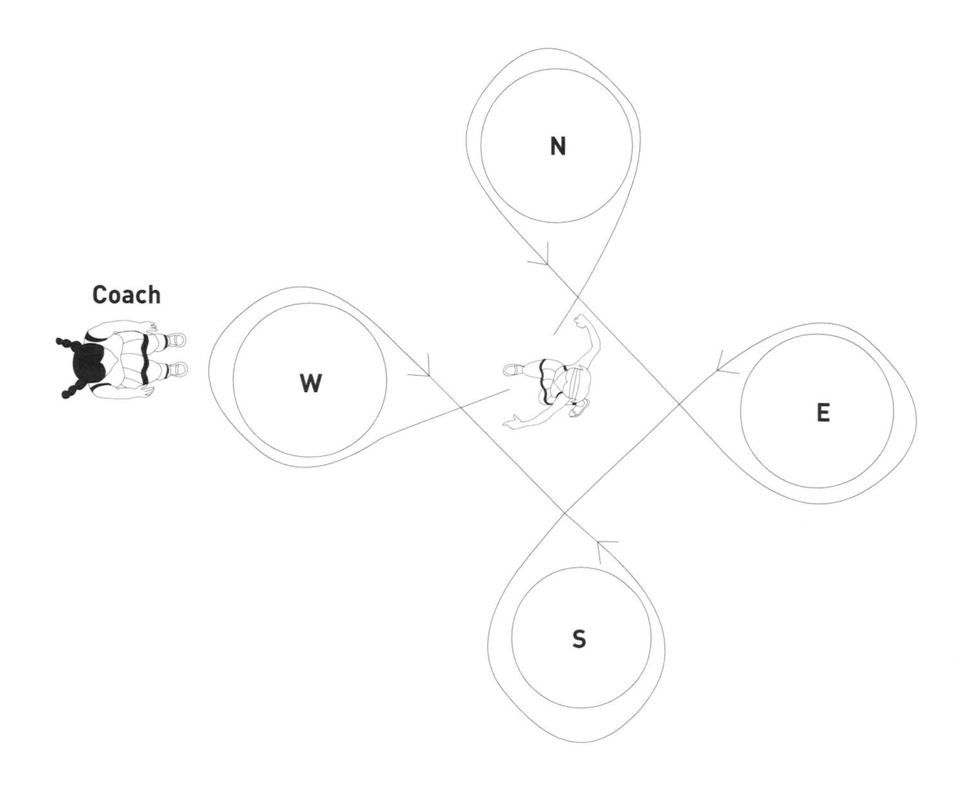

Objective: To condition the body and improve agility.

Equipment: Four hoops designated North, South, East and West.

Description: Lay out the hoops in a compass formation 3 m apart. Player 1 stands in the centre of the compass and on the coach's command (e.g. 'West') runs around that hoop, facing the coach at all times. The player then moves clockwise around the 'compass' until all hoops have been rounded.

Coaching points: Make sure the players face the coach at all times and don't just follow their noses around the hoops. They will have to move sideways and backwards as well as forwards. Hoops are used instead of cones so players have to work around them, as they are too big to just step over.

Progression: This can be made more fun by adapting it to 'wink murder' – when the coach winks the players must run to a beanbag or ball outside the 'compass', pass it under each leg, around their back and then finish with it held on top of their head. The last one to finish is out.

drill 44 *figure 8 drill*

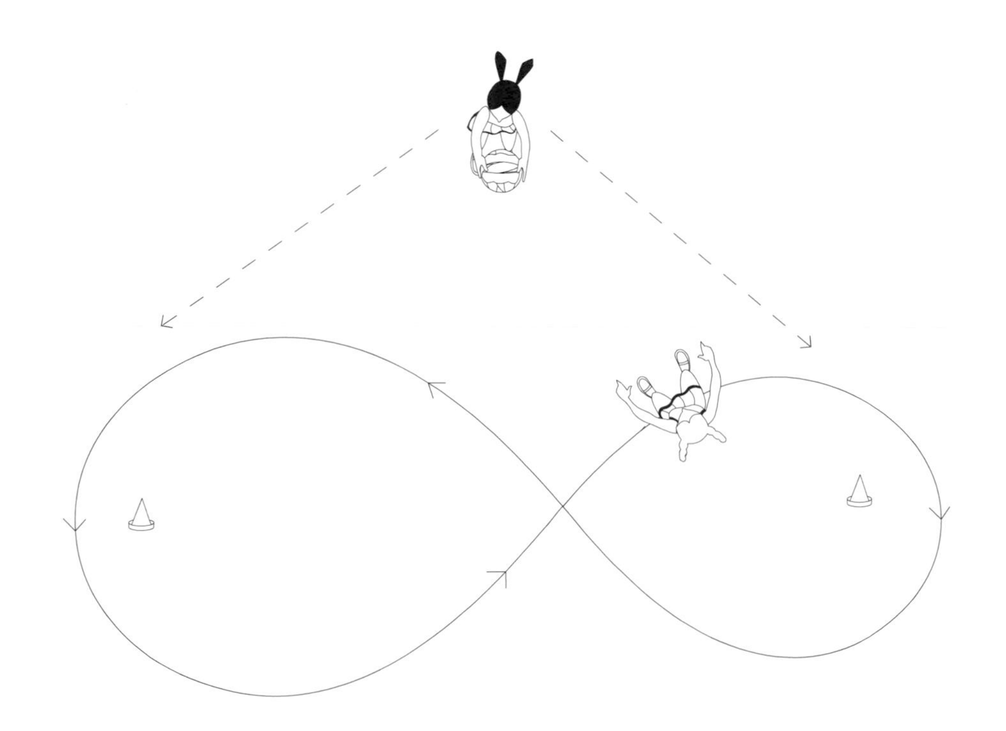

Objective: To improve movement skills and spatial awareness.

Equipment: One ball and two cones between two players.

Description: Set up the cones about 2 m apart. Player 1 stands in front of the two cones. Player 2 runs a figure 8 around the two cones, facing player 1 at all times. In this way player 2 will use a variety of footwork patterns and speeds during the circuit (e.g. quick steps, side steps, cross-overs and so on). At random, player 1 feeds a pass which is received, landed and returned by player 2 before she restarts the circuit.

Coaching points: Watch for players 'following their nose' around the cones. The idea of this drill is that player 2 faces up court and watches the ball at all times. Changes of direction around the cone should be quick and controlled to reduce the time the ball is out of the line of sight and balance must be controlled at all times – if at any time control deteriorates, slow the drill down.

Progression: Move player 1 into different positions to vary the angle of the pass.

drill 45 half-moon drill

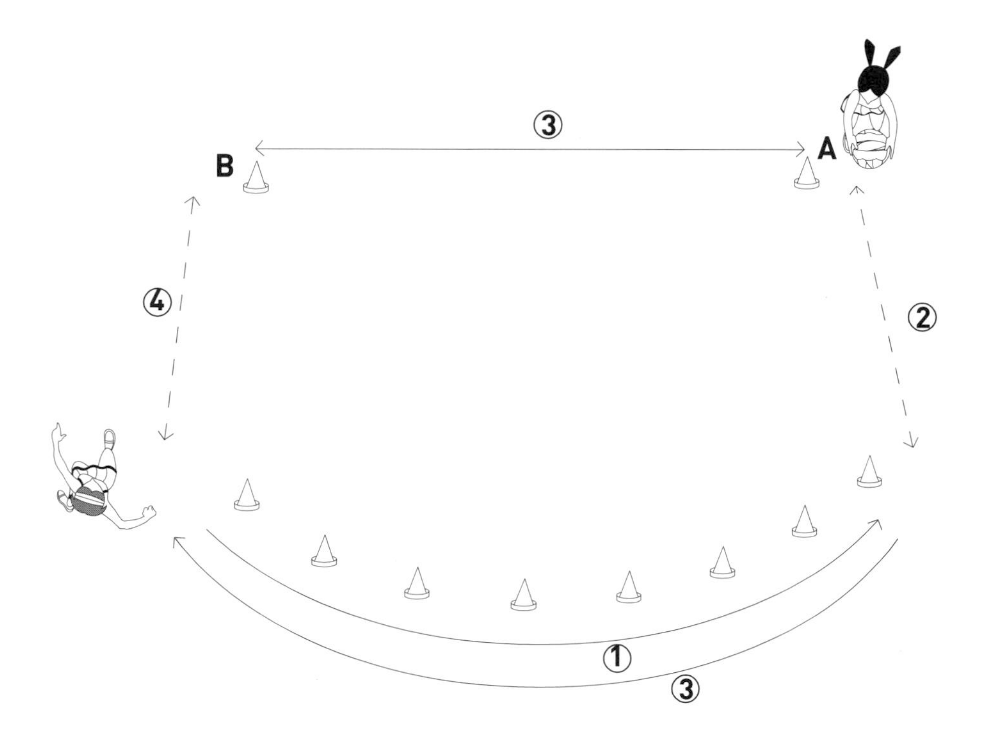

Objective: To develop movement skills and practise passing under pressure.

Equipment: Ten cones and one ball between two players.

Description: Set up eight of the cones in a semi-circle. Two more cones are set 2–3 m back at either end of the semi-circle. On the coach's command player 1 side steps around the cones. When she gets to the end she lands (two-footed), receives and returns a pass from player 2 (standing at A) and then returns to the other side of the semi-circle. By the time they get there, player 2 must have run to B where once again she gives and receives a pass.

Coaching points: This is supposed to be a fast-feet drill so make sure the runner only has a short distance to cover and does not get tired and reduce the quality of her movements. If you use groups of three players, then two can pass and run while the third has one minute to walk slowly around the court to recover.

Progression: Vary the type of passes used.

drill 46 *pivoting practice*

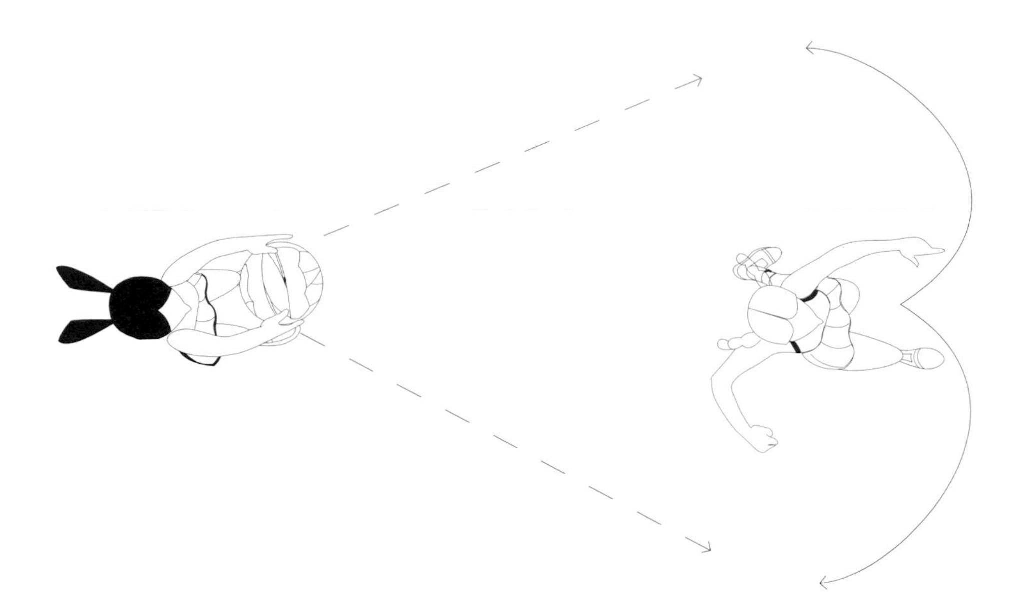

Objective: To practise pivoting.

Equipment: One ball between two players.

Description: Player 1 is working, player 2 is feeding the ball. Player 1 stands with her back to player 2, approximately 3 m away. Player 2 calls 'left' or 'right' to player 1, who pivots to the appropriate side to receive the ball.

Coaching points: Player 1 should start in a balanced position, feet about hip width apart, knees slightly bent and weight on the balls of the feet. Movement should be quick, using little steps, with the hands ready to catch the ball. Players should take turns receiving the ball.

Progression: Vary the type of pass used, for example a high or low ball, bounce pass or pass further away from player 1 so she has to stretch to receive the ball. Player 1 should try to receive the ball in a balanced position rather than at full stretch. The aim is to move the feet quickly; include an extra step if needed to receive the ball.

drill 47 hopscotch passing

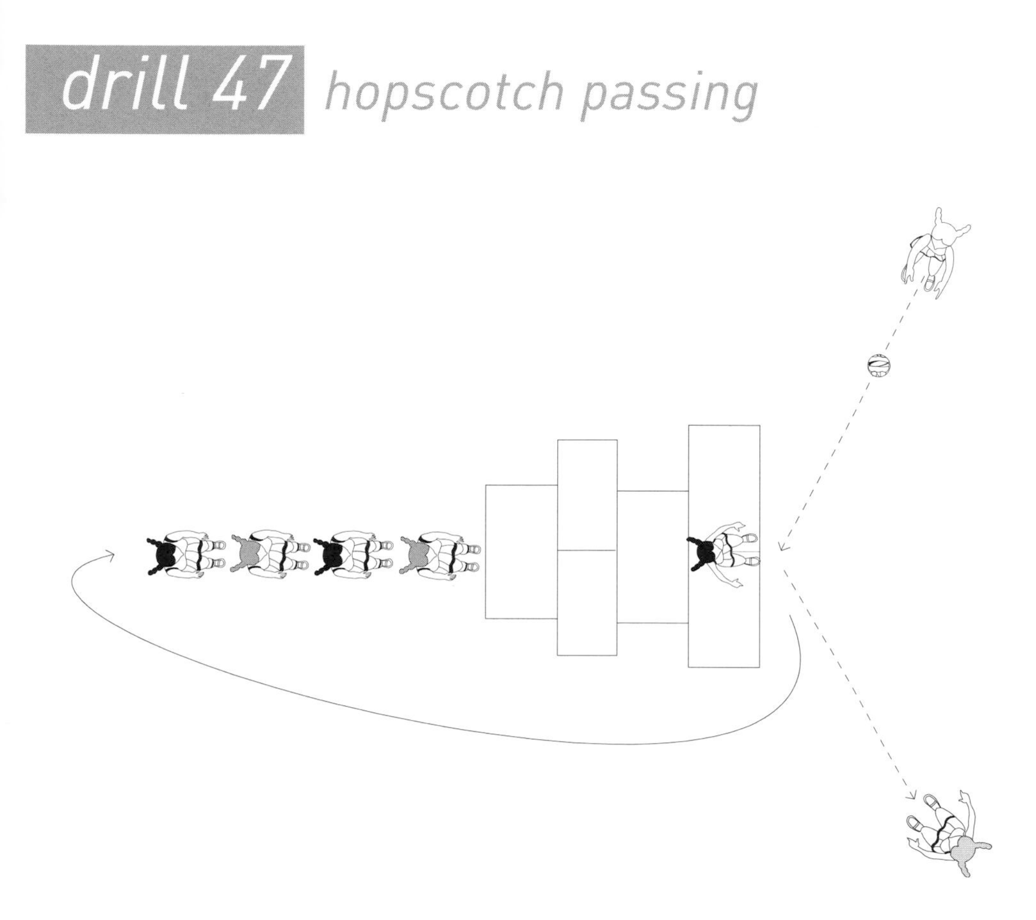

Objective: To develop power and speed using low-level plyometrics.

Equipment: One ball, hopscotch ladder chalked out as shown.

Description: Two feeders stand about 3 m from the end of the ladder, 3 m apart. One of them has a ball. On the coach's command the first player hopscotches down the grid, lands (two-footed) on the last squares and receives a chest pass from the feeder. The player returns the ball to the other feeder. When the feeder has control of the ball, the player runs straight back down the grid, high-fives the next player and goes to the back of the queue.

Coaching points: This is a fast-feet drill as much as a passing practice. Ensure that the players hit every step or hop accurately and treat the squares as if they are red hot. (With younger players speed should be built up slowly.)

Progression: Set up a timed team race – how long does it take to get everyone through? With two teams, set up a race. As the players gain confidence, widen the distance between the feeders to introduce a pivot between receiving and giving the pass.

drill 48 perpetual marking

Objective: To improve awareness and communication; to practise passing under pressure.

Equipment: One ball, six markers between six players.

Description: Set up an area equivalent to about one third of a court. Divide the players into two teams – attackers have the ball and defenders have to try and intercept it. Players must not pass back to the player from whom they receive the ball. When the ball gets intercepted or a pass is lost, the groups swap roles.

Coaching points: Encourage accuracy of passing and lots of communication. Don't let fatigue lead to a sloppy practice. One minute of intense running is a lot! Use the rest at the changeover of roles to reaffirm objectives.

Progression: Four players per team with two balls means that players need to raise awareness as there will be two active balls at any one time. If you have an exceptional group of players then you can try two balls and three players per team!

drill 49 shadowing

Objective: To encourage concentration and fast reactions.

Equipment: One ball, one third of the court.

Description: Spread the players out at least 2 m apart. The coach stands at the front of the area with a ball, with all of the players facing him or her. On the coach's command, players start 'fast feet' running on the spot and shadow or mirror the moves the coach makes. At first, the coach moves the ball to the left, right, front, up, down, but can also toss the ball up for the players to jump and 'catch', or drop the ball to either side for the players to stoop and 'collect'.

Coaching points: Keep the movements coming thick and fast once the group is working. Short, sharp sessions with rests in between are recommended.

Progression: When the coach signals, the players must sprint to a predetermined point and return to their starting point. For more confusion set four bases using coloured cones; when the coach shouts a colour the players must sprint to the relevant base.

drill 50 blocking drill

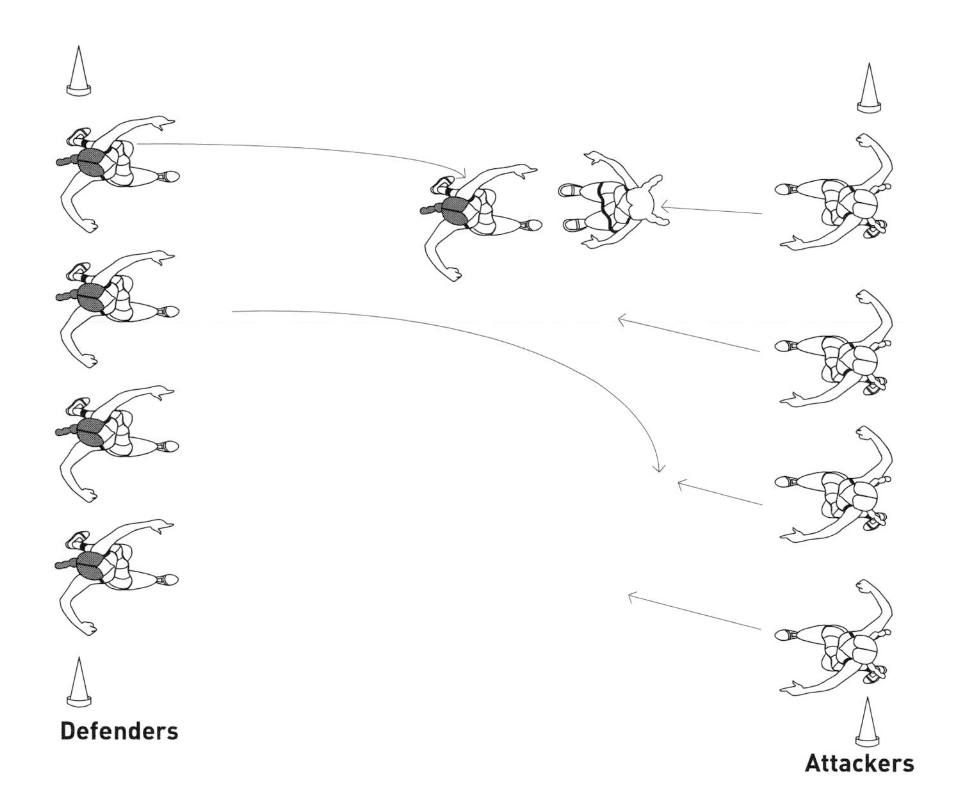

Objective: To develop blocking/zoning skills.

Equipment: Six cones.

Description: Use the cones to mark out a reasonably large area, maximum size two thirds of the court. Split the players into two groups. One group are the attackers (As) and the second group are the defenders (Ds). Ds line up behind one base line and As line up on the other base line, opposite their D partner. The coach gives all As a number and then calls out two numbers at a time. Those two As run and try to get 'home' behind the defenders' base line. The D partners try and block them out of the area for as long as possible. The Ds can work together and do not have to only zone their partner.

Coaching points: Watch for contact at all times and encourage communication. The presence of more than one attacker at a time provides an authentic game environment, but beware of too many players in too small a space.

Progression: Start with one-on-one sessions, then introduce the second pair.

drill 51 hoop drills

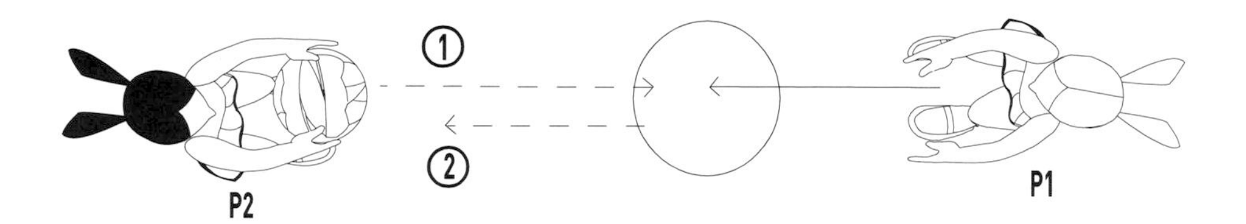

Objective: To develop landing and passing skills.

Equipment: One ball, one hoop (or equivalent).

Description: Player 1 runs towards the hoop, receives a pass from player 2 and completes a two-footed landing in the hoop. She then passes back to the feeding player and runs back to the start position.

Coaching points: Concentrate on one element at a time (particularly with younger players) as you introduce the drill. Perform the run and land initially and then, when everyone has mastered that, introduce the ball.

Progression: There are an infinite number of progressions to this drill as the angle of feed and run can be varied to simulate game situations. For example, player 1 can run, receive a pass, land, perform a half pivot, then pass; or run at an angle to the hoop, receive, land on the outside foot, do a half pivot, return the pass.

drill 52 cones drill

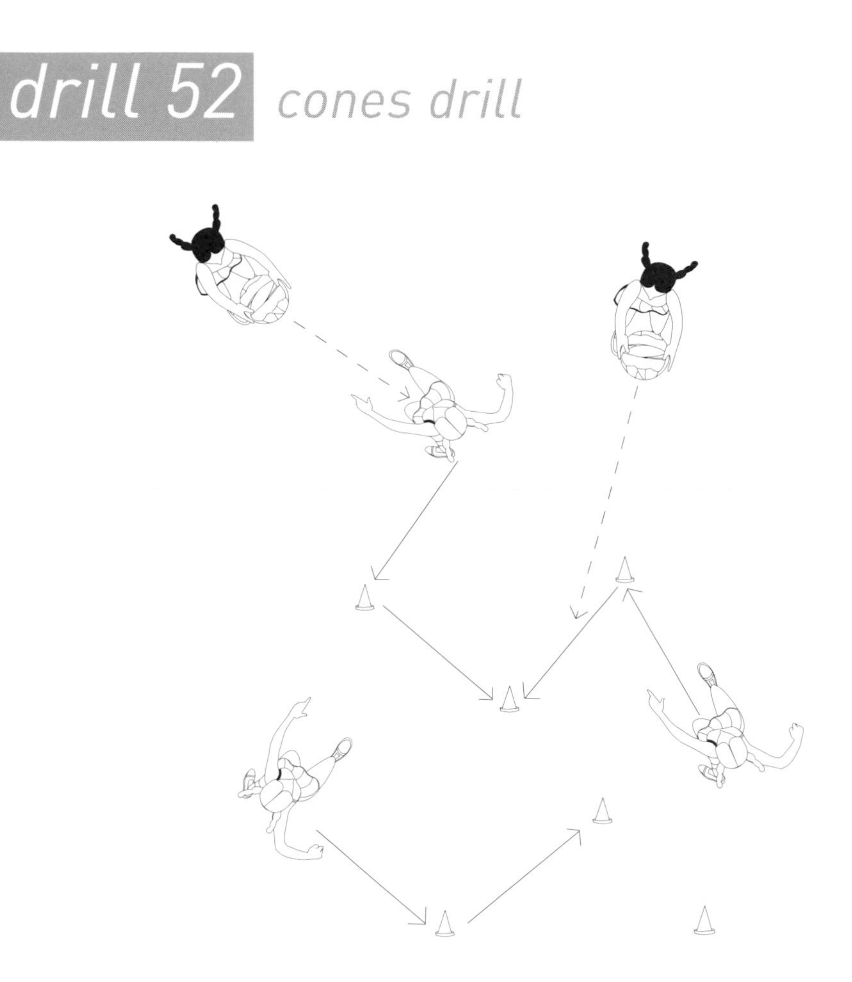

Objective: To strengthen and ingrain sharp changes of direction.

Equipment: Two cones per player (this drill needs at least eight players), and two balls.

Description: Cones are spread randomly over one third of the court. Two players are feeders (F) and stand at the head of the area. The other players run to a cone and push off hard to another, watching the feeders at all times. At will, the feeders pass a ball to a player who receives, lands and returns a pass to the other feeder. (Players may have to pivot to do this.)

Coaching points: Players have to keep their heads up so they don't run into anyone. Limit the length of the drill to 30 seconds and then change the feeders. This means the runners can have a rest every other time. Look for quick and controlled changes of direction, which are achieved by pushing off on the outside foot using the arms and shoulders for balance.

Progression: Introduce more runners.

drill 53 footwork patterns

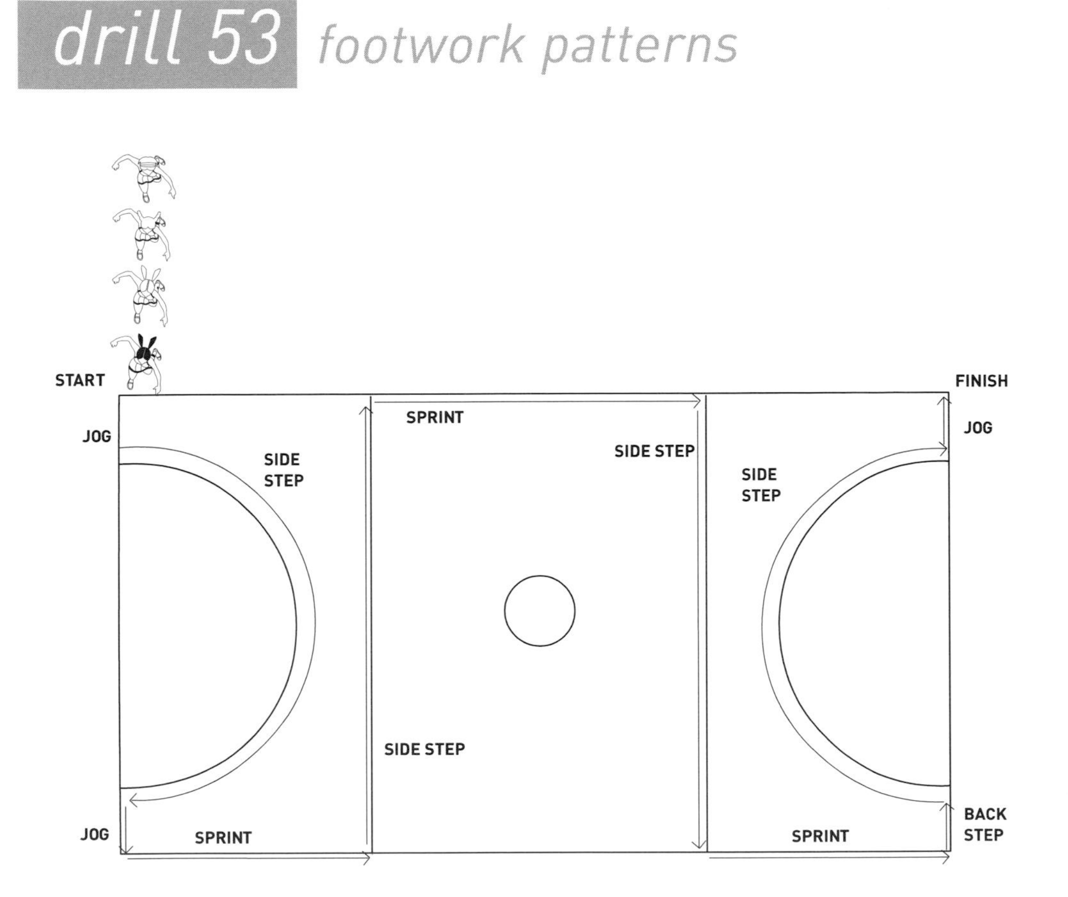

Objective: To practise different footwork steps.

Equipment: The whole court.

Description: Starting at one corner of the base line players follow each other using the following steps and footwork patterns around the court. Jog along the base line up to the circle, side step around the circle, then jog the remainder of the baseline. At the side line change direction and sprint to the third line, sidestep along the third line to the opposite side, then sprint from the third line to the next third line. Side step across the court on the third line, sprint to the base line, backward-steps to the circle line and side step around the circle. Jog the remainder of the base line before finishing in the corner vertically opposite the start.

Coaching points: The aim is to keep the weight balanced, moving forwards with quick changes of direction pushing off from the outside foot.

Progression: Introduce cross steps around the circle edge. Cross steps involve a sideways movement with one foot crossing over the front of the other.

drill 54 ladder passing

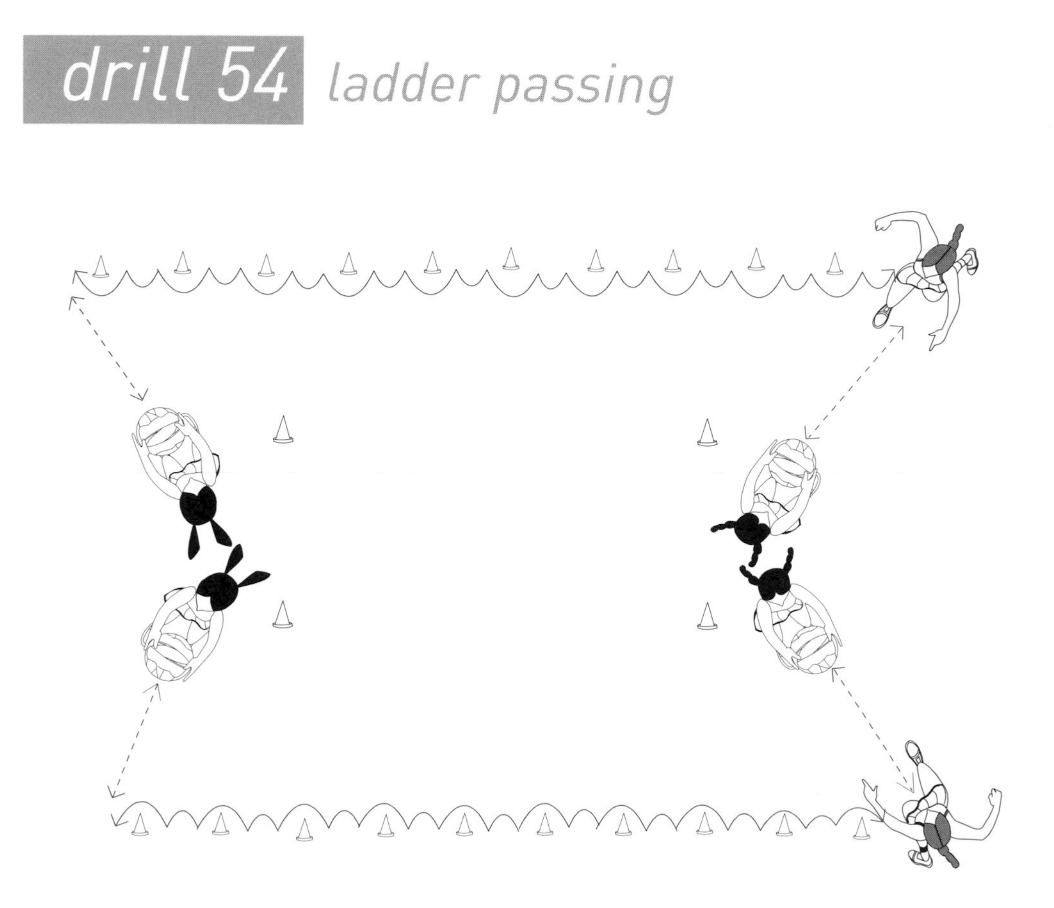

Objective: To develop movement skills and practise passing under pressure.

Equipment: 22 cones and four balls between six players.

Description: Set up two lines of ten cones 5 m apart, with about 30 cm between cones. Two more cones are set in between the rows at either end (A and B) with two passers back to back at each one. The other two players are the runners, with one standing at the end of each line of cones. On the coach's command the runners side step over the cones hitting every gap with very fast feet. When they get to the end of the line they land (two-footed) to receive and return a ball from a passer, then return to the other end of the row of cones in the same way where another passer waits. Each runner completes four passes and then rests. They score a point for each perfect pass, where the passer does not have to move to catch the ball.

Coaching points: This is a fast-feet drill so ensure plenty of recovery time.

Progression: Vary the type of passes used.

drill 55 triangle drill

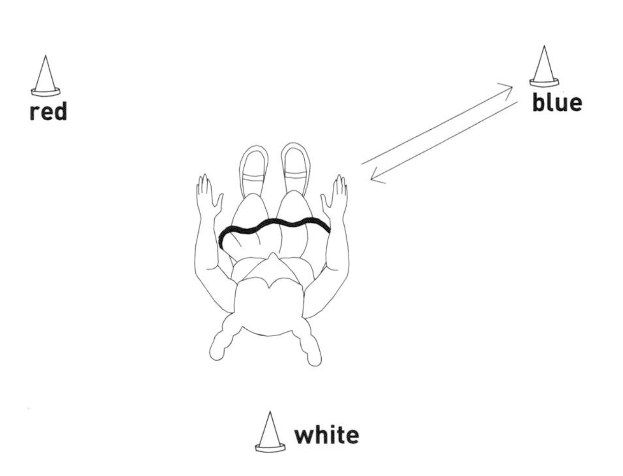

Objective: To practise balance and speed of movement, hand–eye co-ordination, reaction time and concentration.

Equipment: Three different-coloured cones between two players.

Description: Set up the cones to make a triangle, with the cones approximately 2 m apart. Player 1 is working and starts in the centre, and must return there at the end of each movement. Player 2 stands outside the triangle and shouts a colour to player 1, who must then move to the required cone using a variety of footwork patterns. Once she returns to the centre, player 2 shouts another colour.

Coaching points: Look for balanced, quick footwork and changes of direction. Footwork should be small steps, with changes of direction achieved by pushing off on the outside foot to encourage transferral of weight.

Progression: Increase the distance between cones. Add an extra cone to make the working area a 3 m square. Add a ball, with player 2 passing the ball to player 1 as she reaches the cone.

drill 56 box drill

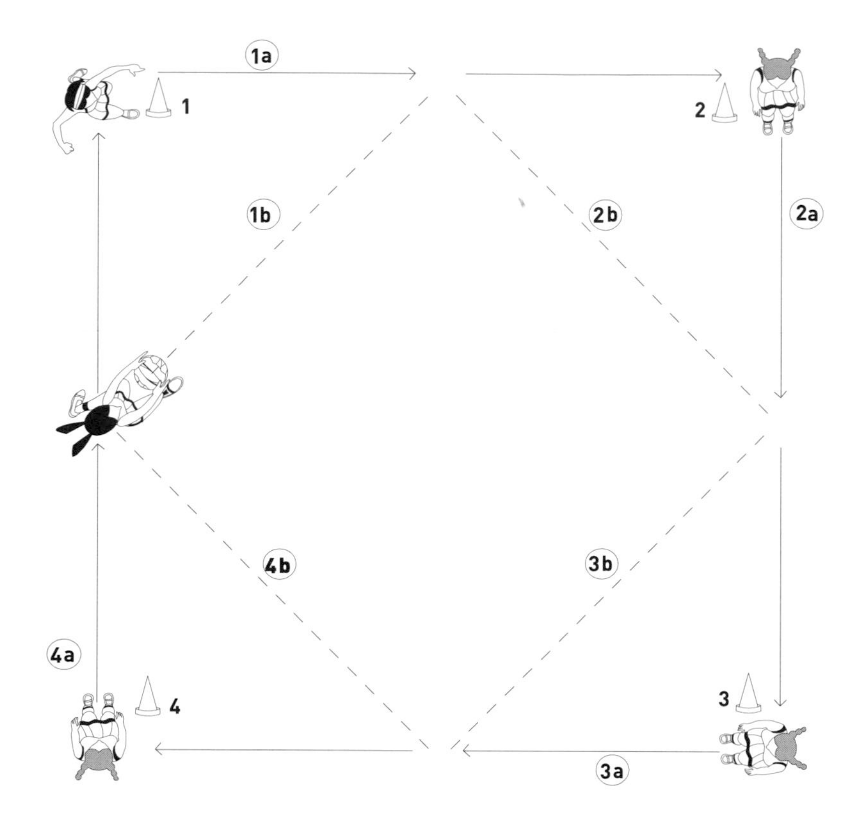

Objective: To practise receiving a pass from an angle.

Equipment: Four cones and one ball between five players.

Description: Place the cones in a 10 m square. Four players stand at a cone, player 1 at cone 1 and so on. The remaining player stands between cone 4 and cone 1 with the ball. On the coach's command player 1 runs towards cone 2 to receive a pass from player 5 halfway between the cones. Player 5 then runs to cone 1 to take up the space vacated by player 1. As soon as player 1 receives the ball, player 2 runs towards cone 3 and player 1 delivers a pass to be received halfway between cones 2 and 3, and runs on to cone 2, and so on.

Coaching points: Ensure players drive out hard for each pass. The pass should be into space and not at a receiver. This is a complex drill that should be walked through initially, so that everyone can then concentrate on passing, landing and pushing off.

Progression: Vary the types of pass. Change the direction of rotation.

ATTACKING AND DEFENDING

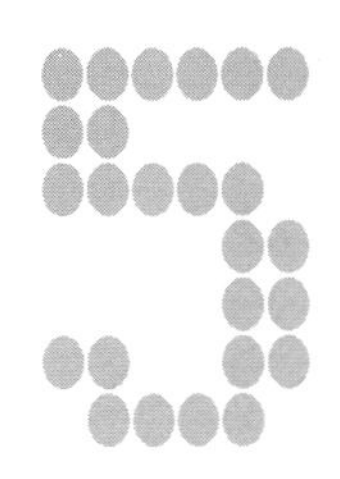

Within this section many of the skills developed previously will be put into a game context. Court and spatial awareness must now be added to passing and movement skills as this is the precursor to pulling all the elements into a structured game play.

Attacking has been paired with defending as the majority of drills that practise one also provide an opportunity to practise the other.

When working on marking skills be aware of where defenders are focusing. It is an understandable habit for defenders to become fixated on what is happening with either the ball or their opponent. To defend one exclusively at the expense of the other is not good practice. Encourage players to think of how they can stay aware of both by marking side-on rather than face-to-face. In the same way attackers can help themselves by becoming aware of the defender's focus.

It is important that players are clear of their primary role and where on court their primary responsibilities lie – their defensive or attacking 'zones'. An awareness of space, and how to create and reduce it, is at the heart of good netball.

drill 57 zoning drill

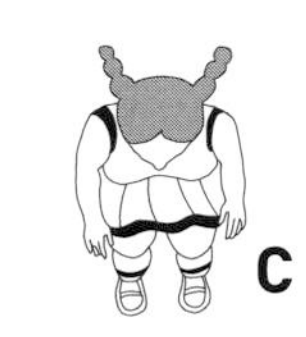

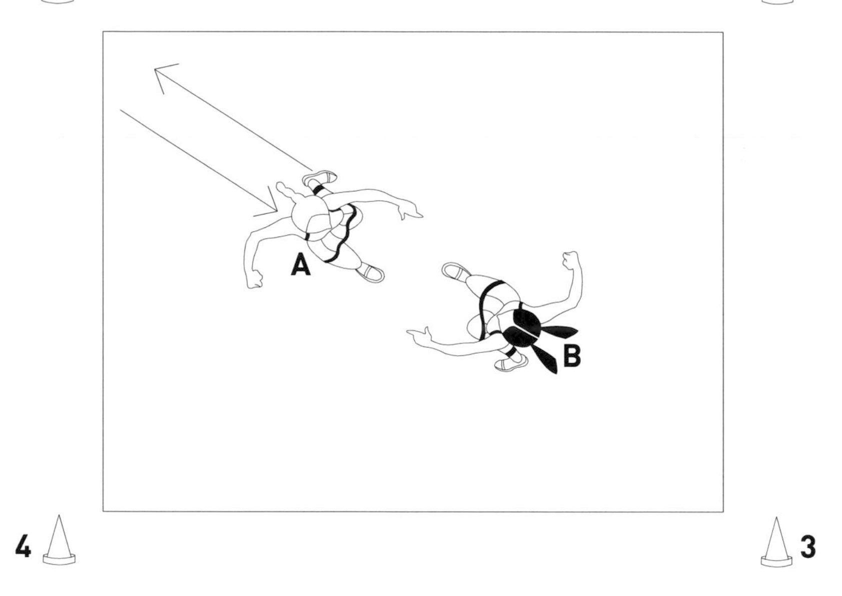

Objective: To develop marking skills.

Equipment: Four cones between three players.

Description: Set up the cones to form a square with 5 m sides. Number the cones 1–4. Player A is an attacker, player B is a defender and player C rests. Players A and B start in the centre of the square face to face, on their toes ready to move. Player C calls out a number and player A must try to get to that cone before player B. Player B tries to zone or block her out without contacting her. After three attempts, rotate positions.

Coaching points: Focus on the ready position – not flat-footed, but ready to go! Ensure that player C knows the rules on contact and acts as umpire during the drill.

Progression: Player C has a ball and player A calls the cone number. Player C has to pass towards the designated cone for player A to receive.

drill 58 top tipping

Objective: To practise interceptions.

Equipment: One ball between three players.

Description: In groups of three A is a feeder and B and C are in competition for the ball. B and C stand side by side about 1 m apart. A throws the ball about 2 m above their heads. B and C jump vertically to try to tip the ball away from the other player and catch it. Players B and C get one point per tip – play best out of five then rotate the players.

Coaching points: Explosive jumping is a key netball skill and helps defenders develop timing. Look for players tipping with the hand closest to the ball to reduce the risk of contact. Players should swap sides to practise tipping with both hands.

Progression: Draw up a matrix so that all players play everyone else with a prize for the most tips. To add an element of conditioning, have five feeders per pair. Feeder 1 feeds the first ball and the moment that the players are back in position feeder 2 feeds, and so on.

drill 59 marking relay

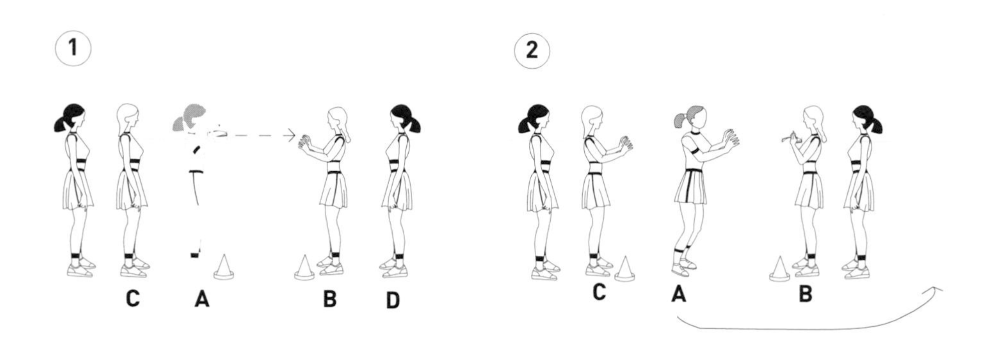

Objective: To practise passing and defensive skills.

Equipment: Two cones and one ball.

Description: Split the players into two groups, who line up facing each other approximately 5 m apart behind two cones. Player 1 starts with the ball and passes ahead to player 2. Player 1 runs to follow the pass and then defends the return pass between players 2 and 3. Once the second pass is made, player 1 runs to the back of the line. Continue until all players have had three runs each, then stop the drill and reaffirm the objectives and key skills before re-starting.

Coaching points: The players can move between the cones but cannot advance beyond them. Discourage lobbed passes but have the players think about different types of passes (bounce passes to beat a tall player and so on).

drill 60 ladder drill

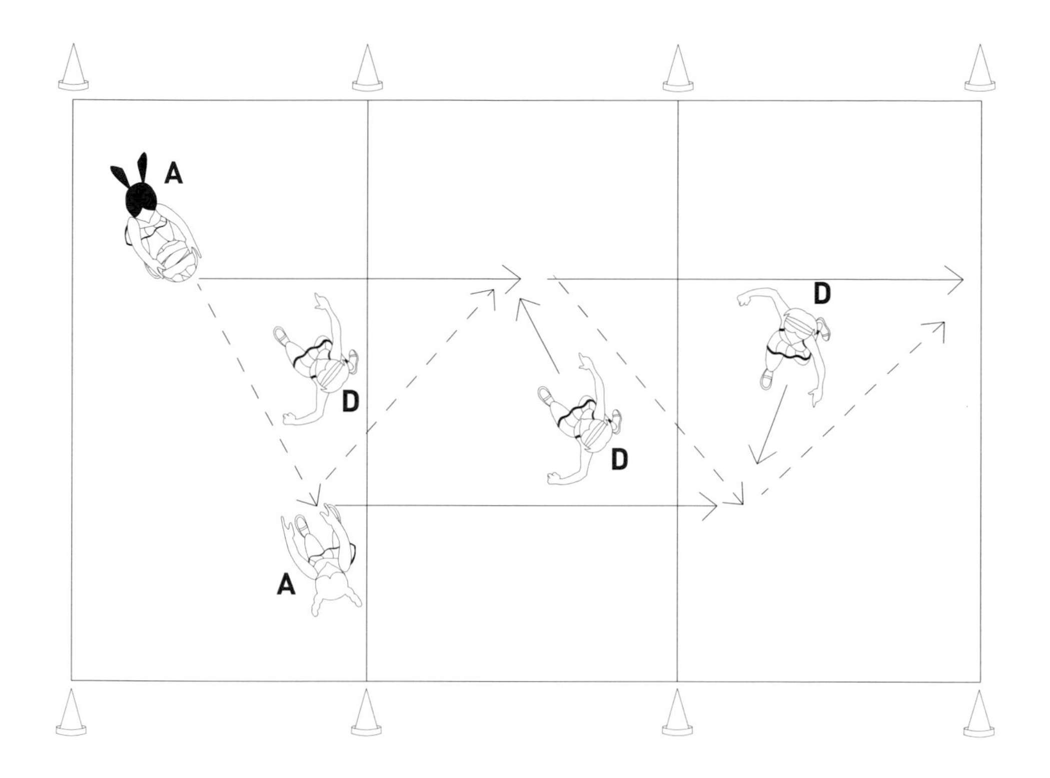

Objective: To improve passing and defensive skills.

Equipment: Eight cones.

Description: Use the cones to set up a grid divided into thirds, each about 5 m by 2.5 m. There should be three defenders and at least two attackers, with one defender per third. The attackers pass the ball to each other along the grid. Each attacker must receive one pass each within each third. The defenders have to try to intercept the ball. If you have extra players, have an extra attacking pair enter the first third once the first pair is clear of it – in this way the drill can be continuous.

Coaching points: Encourage the players to pass the ball into space and create movement in small areas.

Progression: Move the drill into a bigger area and add an extra defender.

drill 61 rollerball

Objective: To introduce the concept of a rolling movement as a form of evasion.

Equipment: Three cones and one ball between two players.

Description: Player 1 is the worker and player 2 is the feeder. Player 1 stands 3–4 m in front of and facing away from player 2, who has the ball. Player 2 calls go and player 1 'rolls' off to the left to receive a pass; as player 1 rolls she must quickly make eye contact with player 2 and only then can the pass be made. The pass is received with a good landing and returned. Player 1 returns to the starting position and the the drill is repeated to the right. This is one repetition. Perform three repetitions and then swap roles.

Coaching points: Ensure the worker pushes off from the correct foot and moves out to meet the ball rather than 'crabbing' sideways.

Progression: Vary the type of pass to include lob, chest, shoulder and bounce. Vary the direction and length of pass (short left or long right) so that the worker must run on to, reverse or jump to receive the ball.

drill 62 passing into space

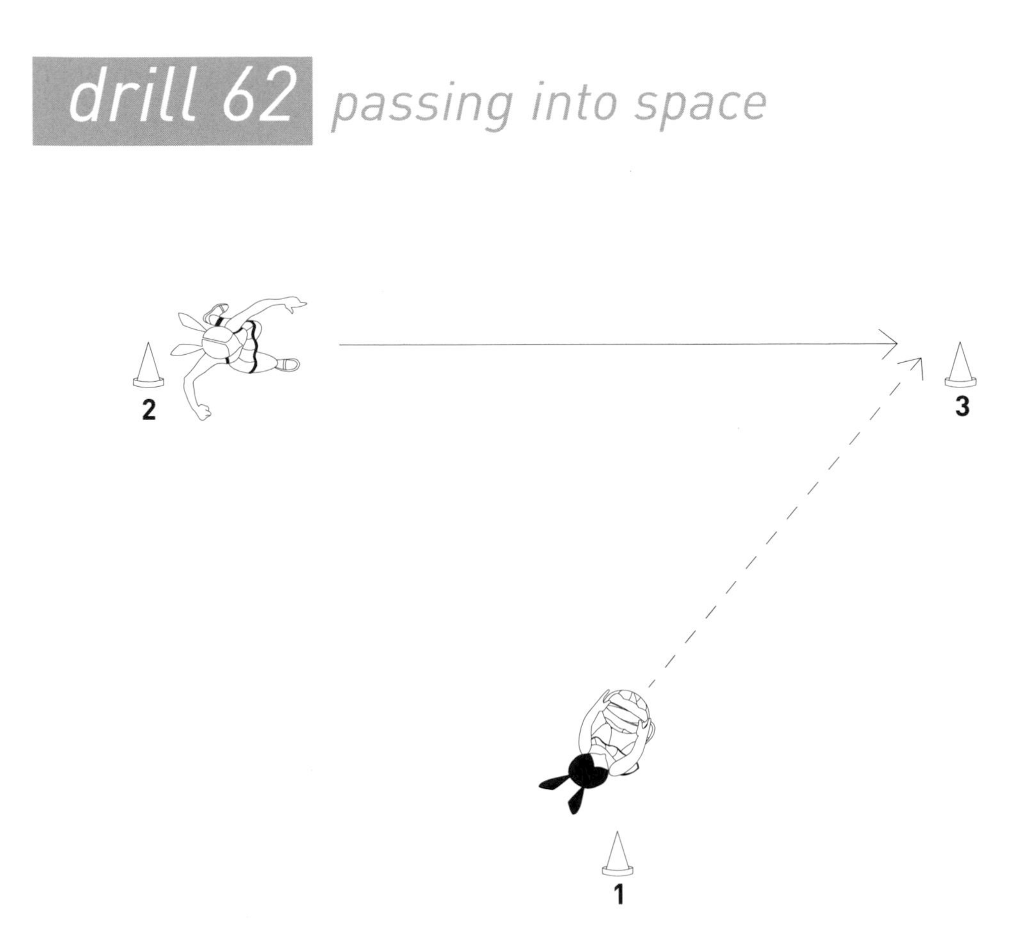

Objective: To practise passing a ball to a moving player, moving into a space to receive a ball and landing correctly to get ready to pass the ball to the next player.

Equipment: One ball and three cones between two players.

Description: Set out the 3 cones approximately 3 m apart to form a triangle. Player 1 stands at cone 1 with the ball. Player 2 starts at cone 2 and must move to receive the pass from player 1 at cone 3. Player 2 sprints to cone 3; player 1 has to time her pass for player 2 to receive the ball as she reaches the cone.

Coaching points: The pass needs to be in front of player 2 so she is running on to the ball. Player 2 should land without stepping and be ready to make the next pass.

Progression: When players are more confident and able to feed and release accurate passes, a third player can be introduced to receive a pass from player 2. Player 3 should stand ready to receive the ball once player 2 has landed. Her position can be varied to include pivoting movements from player 2 so she can make an accurate, balanced pass to player 3.

drill 63 shadows

Objective: To practise marking another player.

Equipment: Two players.

Description: Players 1 and 2 stand next to each other. Player 1 moves around the court using different steps and directions i.e. side step, backwards, forwards and so on, moving quickly and slowly. Player 2 has to stay as close to her partner as possible. Change over when the whistle blows.

Coaching points: The aim is to keep as close to your partner as possible, like a shadow, following her movements.

drill 64 interceptor 1

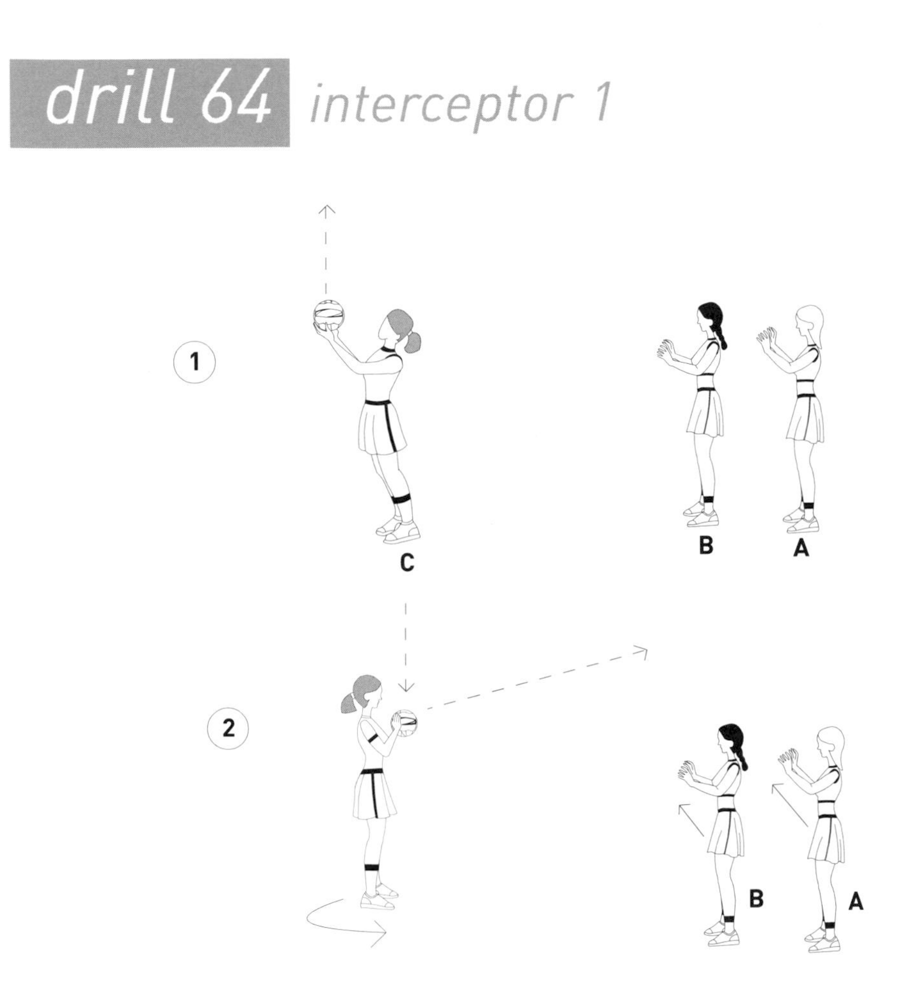

Objective: To improve communication, movement and defensive skills.

Equipment: One ball between three players.

Description: Player A stands behind player B, the defender. Player C stands with her back to the other players, holding the ball. Player C throws the ball in the air, catches it and pivots to throw to player A. Player A indicates which way she is going to move: left, right or overhead. Player C must throw the ball without hesitating and player B tries to intercept the pass.

Coaching points: Attackers should use hand as well as verbal signals to indicate direction of feed. Player C can try using eye-feints to try to throw off the defender. The defender should stand slightly sideways on to the attacker so that she can keep one eye on both players instead of 'ball watching'. Look for players on their toes, attentive and ready to receive or intercept the pass.

Progression: Vary the type of pass. Introduce a second defensive player to defend the pass made by player C.

drill 65 give and go drill

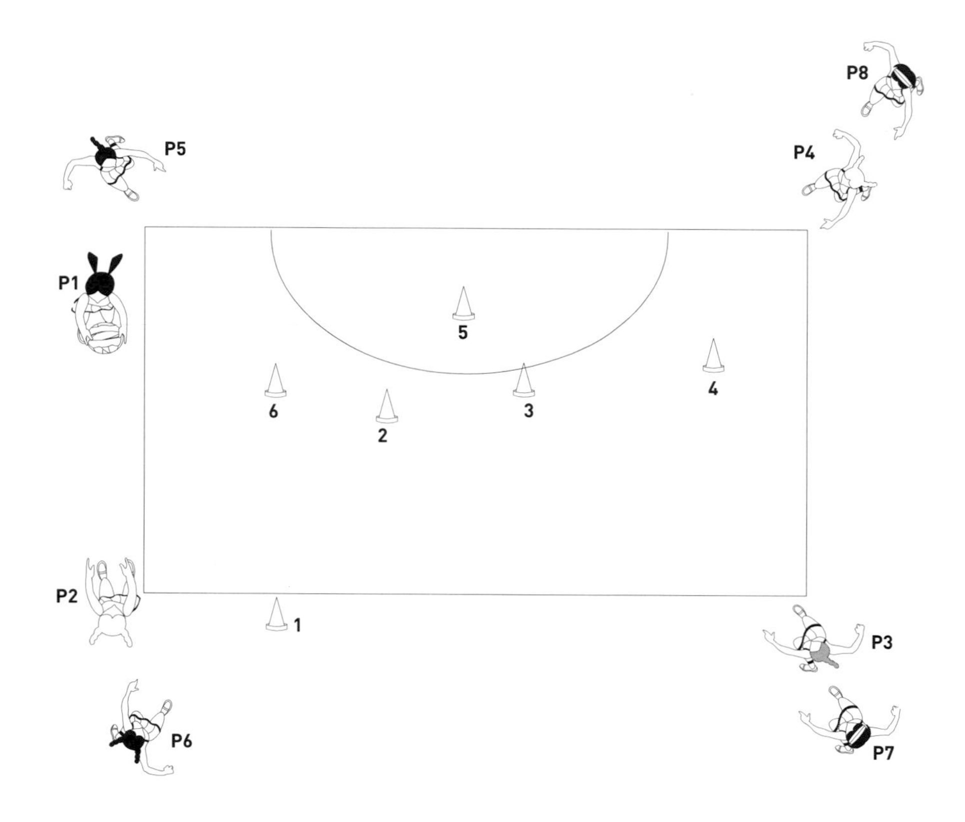

Objective: To develop team skills in the attacking third.

Equipment: One ball, six cones.

Description: Set out the cones in the goal third as shown above. The ball starts with player 1, who passes to player 2. Player 1 then drives to take a chest pass at cone 1. Player 2 drives towards the circle to take a shoulder pass at cone 2. Player 3 drives to take a chest pass at the top of the circle at cone 3. Meanwhile, player 4 has driven towards the post and then out of the circle to take a quick pass at cone 4, which she returns to player 3, and then drives back towards the post to take a high pass at cone 5. Player 5 then drives to cone 6 to take a shoulder pass. She then passes the ball to player 6 and the drill continues. Players move along one starting position after they have completed their section.

Coaching points: This is an advanced drill and should be reserved for older and more experienced players. Walk the drill through first.

Progression: You can advance this drill by adding more balls.

drill 66 British bulldogs

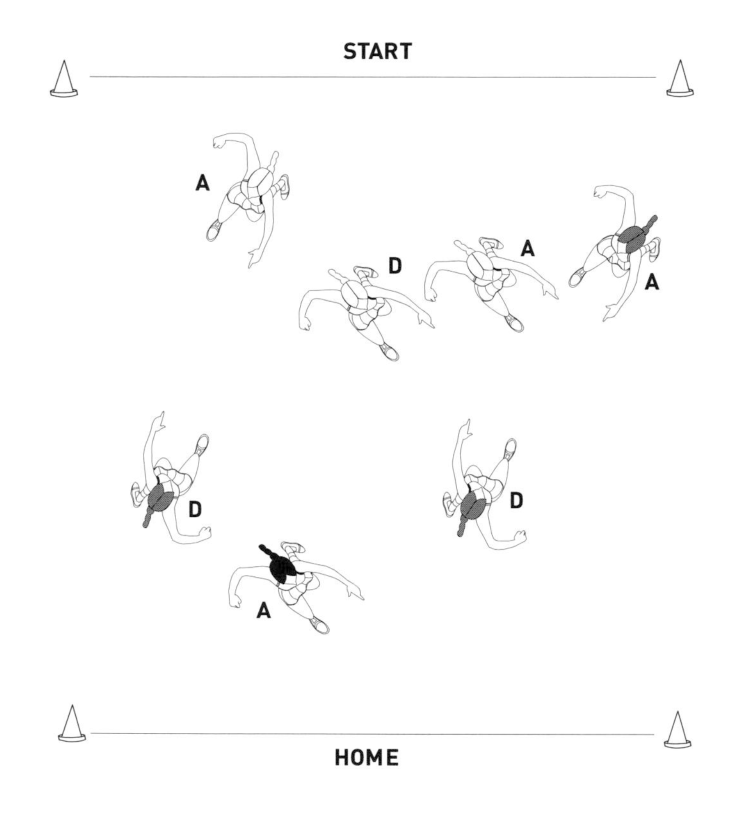

Objective: To develop zone marking skills.

Equipment: One ball and four cones.

Description: Use the cones to mark out an area equivalent to two thirds of a court. Split the group so there are three defenders (D) and as many attackers (A) as you wish. The As start at one end of the area and their objective is to make it to the 'home' line behind the defenders. The Ds try to zone the As to stop them achieving this. Ds must not advance over the centre line. If an A player has been effectively zoned they then become a D. Repeat until there is only one player remaining.

Coaching points: Encourage plenty of communication between defenders. This is a team skill.

Progression: Introduce a ball. Players not zoned must pass and can only hold possession for three seconds. If they do not make a pass in time then they become a D.

drill 67 block clock

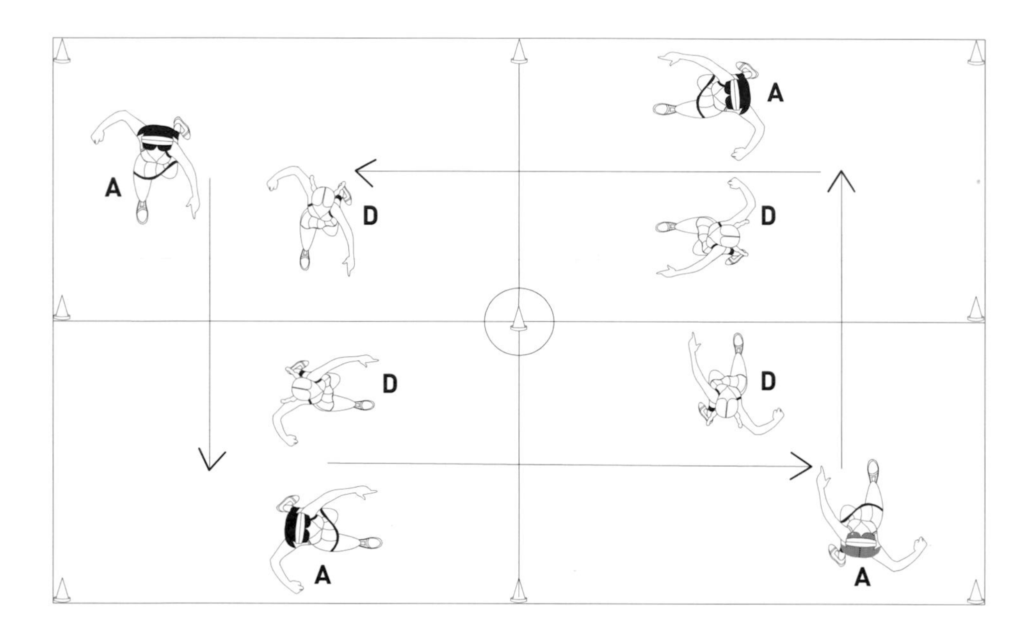

Objective: To introduce blocking out and zone defences.

Equipment: Nine cones.

Description: Use the cones to lay out a grid as shown above in one third of the court. Divide the group into four attackers (As) and four defenders (Ds). Each defender has their own grid area to defend and they must stay there throughout the drill. On the coach's command, the As have to try to get into the next D's area, moving anti-clockwise.

Coaching points: Allocate a set amount of time (say 20 seconds) and then stop the drill. Whether or not the As were successful they then rotate into the next square around and prepare for the next attempt.

Progression: Add a feeder who stands in the centre with a ball and feeds a pass to any A at random. A catches and returns the ball and Ds try to intercept. This is a good opportunity for Ds to experiment by staying off the A to tempt the pass and then try to anticipate and intercept the ball.

drill 68 interceptor 2

Objective: To practise timing when intercepting a ball.

Equipment: One ball between three players.

Description: Players 2 and 3 stand facing each other 3 m apart, chest passing to each other. Player 1 stands behind player 2 and tries to intercept the pass, timing her run around player 2 to avoid contact and reach the ball first.

Coaching points: All players should be on their toes and be ready to move. Player 1 must time her move to intercept the pass.

Progressions: Vary the type of pass. Lengthen the distance of the pass. The interceptor can move to intercept the ball by jumping around the shoulders of the static catcher, landing to catch the ball. At its most advanced, this practice can be set up for the working player to intercept consecutive passes between the feeders. The distance between the feeders should be kept to 3 m for this to work well.

drill 69 marking drill

Objective: To practise dodging to get free from a defender and to practise marking.

Equipment: One ball between three players.

Description: Player A stands behind player B, the defender. Player C stands with the ball facing the other players. Player A must dodge to get free and receive a pass from player C. Player B must try to stick with player A to prevent her receiving the ball.

Coaching points: Look for player A making a definite dodge and indicating where she wants to receive the pass. Eventually, this movement should involve a quick change in direction by pushing off on one foot and using the shoulders to keep the weight moving in the direction in which the player wants to go. Check the position of the defender, who should be marking her player while facing the ball, standing slightly sideways. Her movements should be quick, small side steps to keep up with the attacker. Player C must be ready to pass the ball to player A as soon as she is free.

Progression: Vary the type of pass.

drill 70 piggy in the middle

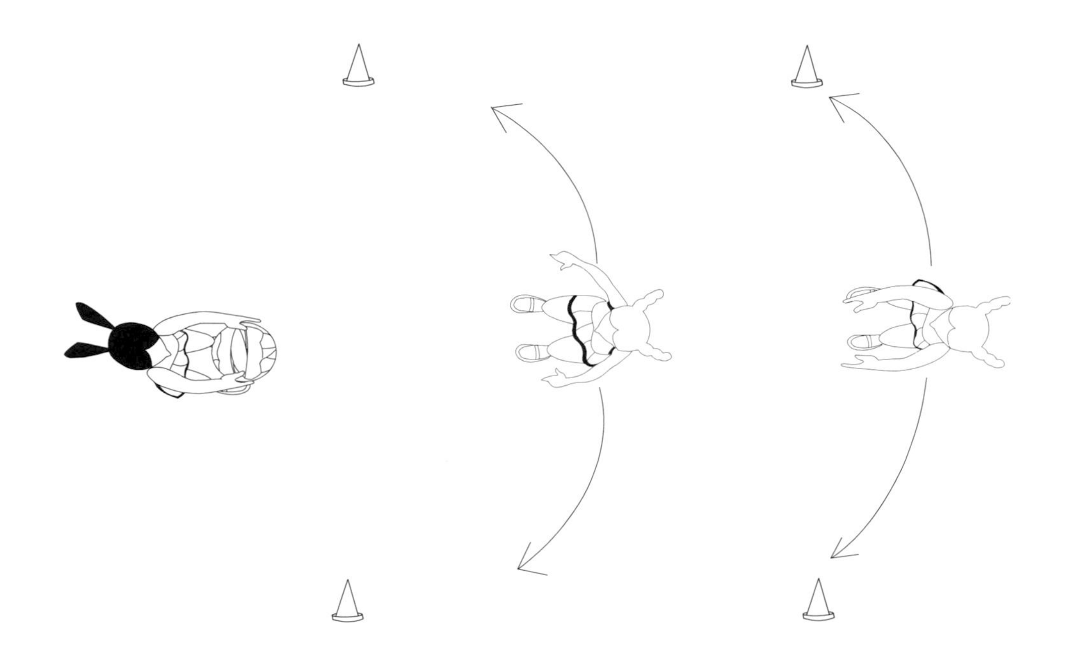

Objective: To practise passing and receiving the ball, getting free and defending the ball.

Equipment: Four cones and one ball between three players.

Description: Mark out a small square with the cones. The space should be sufficient to allow some sideways movement but should also restrict the players. The three players stand in the middle of the square in a straight line. Players 1 and 2, the attackers, pass the ball to each other. Player 3, the defender, standing in between players 1 and 2, tries to intercept the pass.

Coaching points: The attackers should try to use small side steps to make it easier for their partner to make an accurate pass.

Progression: This simple drill can be advanced by introducing another defender. With two defenders marking the ball, the attackers will need to move quickly into a space to receive a pass.

drill 71 piggies in the middle

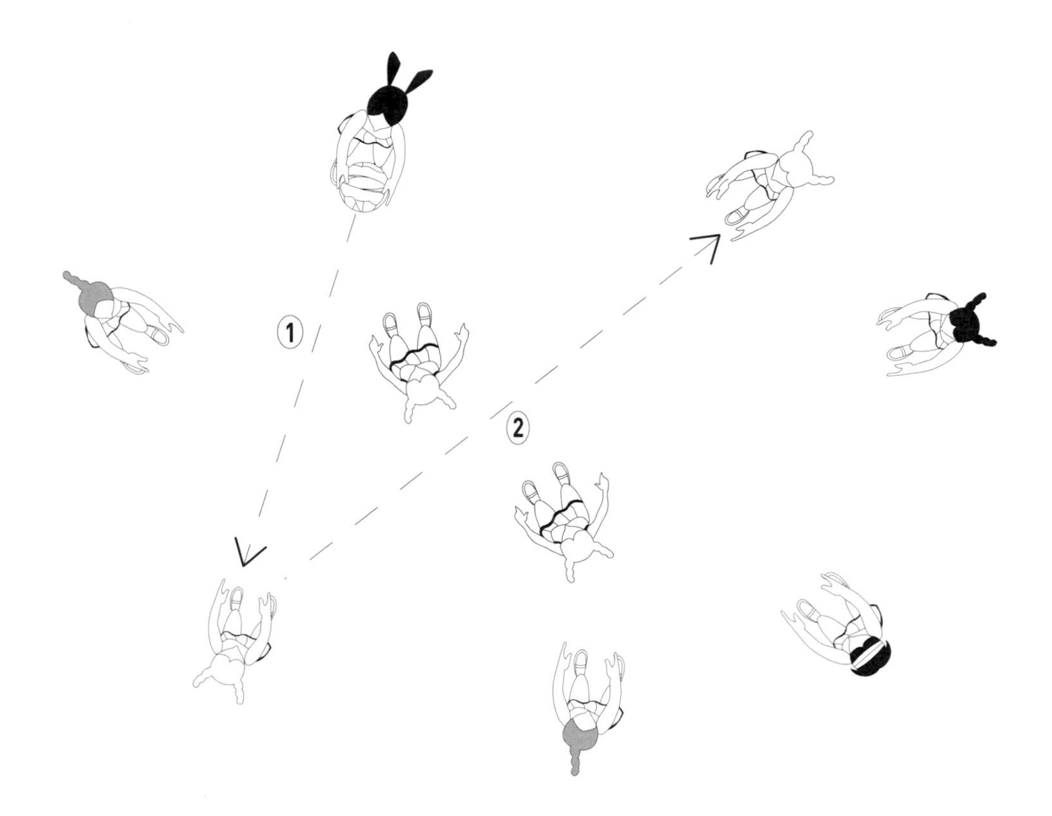

Objective: To practise passing and defensive skills.

Equipment: One ball between seven players.

Description: Form the group into a circle with two players in the centre. The ball is moved across the circle at varying speeds and heights using various types of passes. The players in the middle of the circle try to intercept the ball. Change players after a certain number of passes (start with twenty). The 'piggies' keep score of how many touches (one point), knock-downs (three points) or catches (ten points) they make.

Coaching points: Passers must call the name of the person to whom they are passing. Look for quick, accurate passing.

Progression: Try asking the passers to communicate without speaking. Receivers have to signal for the ball (left, right, up, down and so on). Passers can experiment with eye-feints – look at one player and pass to another (very common in basketball but not so common in netball).

drill 72 triangle drill

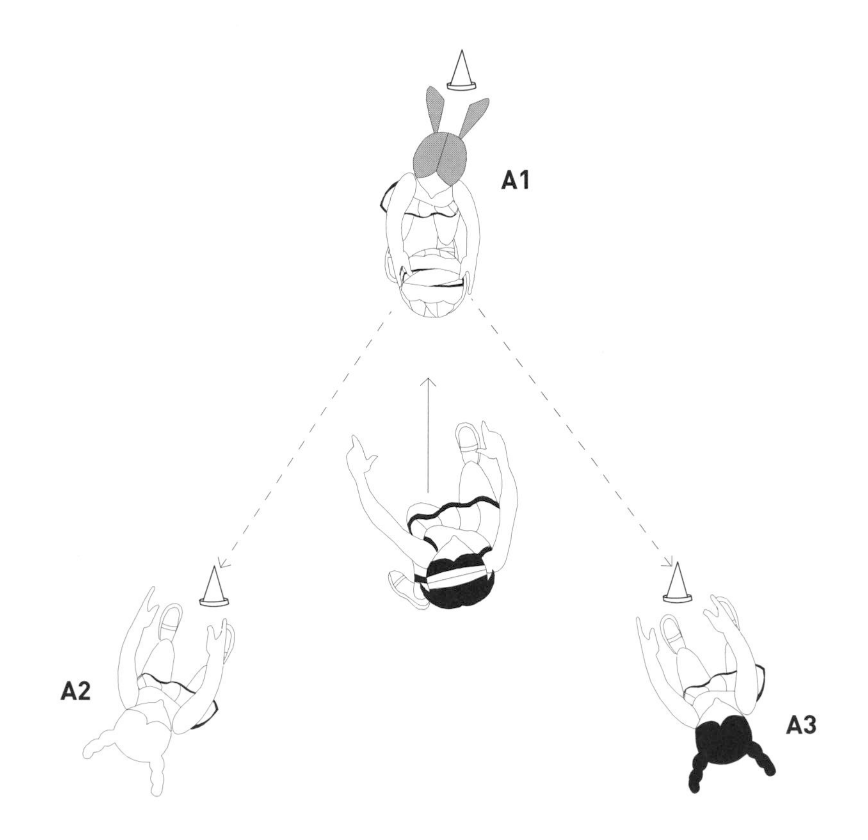

Objective: To practise passing and defensive skills.

Equipment: One ball and three cones between four players.

Description: Use the cones to mark out a triangle with sides of approximately 4 m. One player stands on each point of the triangle – these are the attackers, or As. A1 has the ball. The fourth player stands opposite the ball, defending A1's pass to A2 and A3. The defender keeps score of how many touches (one point), knock-downs (three points) or catches (10 points) they make. Rotate the players so there is a new defender and a new passer.

Coaching points: Ensure good fast chest passes or bounce passes, not overhead passes. Encourage the defender to think and talk about what they are watching – the ball or the passer's eyes? They should always react to the ball, not the eyes.

Progression: Adjust the distances between the attackers according to skill and size of the defender to ensure she has a realistic chance of intercepting the ball.

drill 73 cut the cake

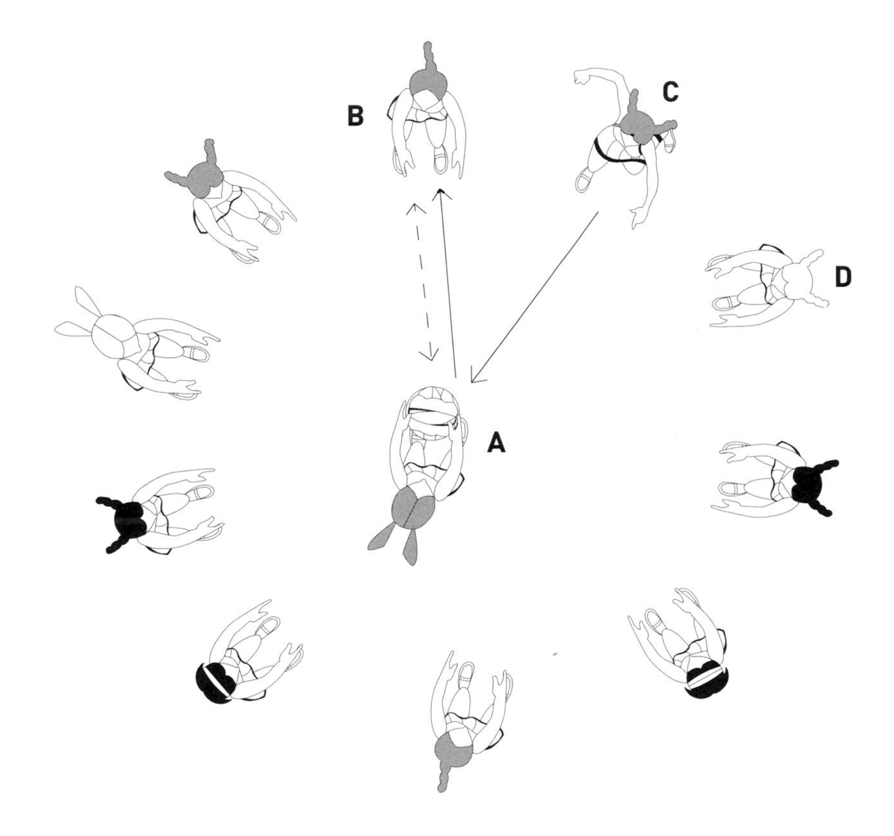

Objective: To practise passing and defensive skills.

Equipment: One ball between eight players.

Description: Form a circle with one player in the middle. A is in the centre of the circle and has the ball. A passes to one of the players in the circle (B), then runs to defend B's pass. The player next to B, player C, runs into the middle of the circle and receives a pass from B, which A tries to intercept. C then passes the ball to the next player in the circle (D) and runs to defend. Repeat until all the players have been in the middle.

Coaching points: Watch spacing with the defenders. Encourage lots of energy, movement and communication. Insist on good quality passes at all times.

drill 74 big pig

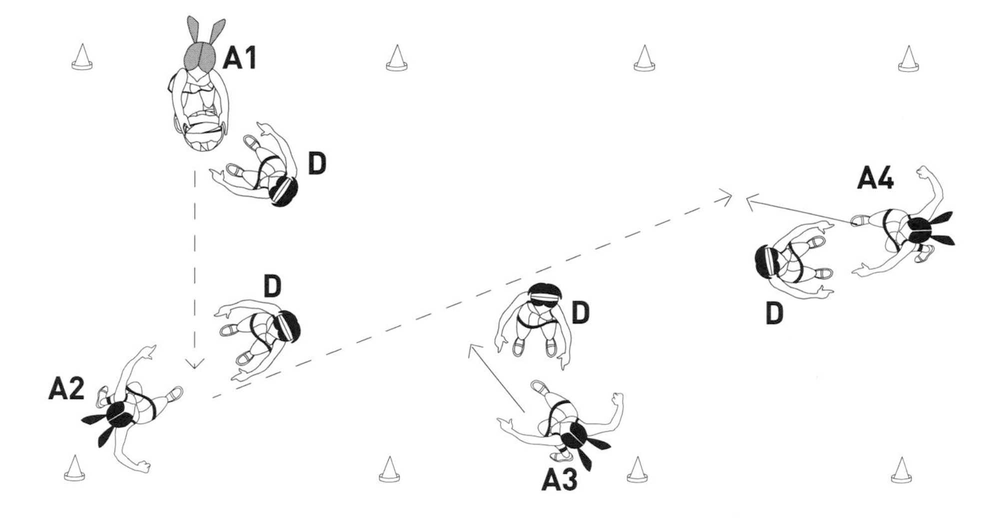

Objective: To develop spatial awareness, and practise passing and marking.

Equipment: One ball, one third of the court, bibs.

Description: Divide the players into two teams, with one team wearing the bibs. One team tries to complete six consecutive passes. The defending team tries to gain possession. Possession also changes with a dropped ball and any infringements set by the coach, for example the ball going out of bounds, footwork and excessively short passes. Passes cannot be returned to the same player.

Coaching points: Defending players can experiment with different types of marking and can also try laying off attackers to try and draw a pass, which they can then try to intercept. The key element is to pass into a space to which a player is moving, not to where they are currently standing.

Progression: Reduced space increases the pressure on the attackers. The drill can be developed by asking the attackers to progress from one side of the court to the other with the defenders trying to stop them. Change the type of pass.

Catherine Cox (the Swifts, Australia) demonstrates good shooting technique, using a flick of the wrist to add backspin.

SHOOTING

Shooting is a very specific skill requiring accuracy, good balance, controlled movements and confidence in the shooting circle. Most young players want to be Goal Shooter (GS) or Goal Attack (GA) but often are complacent in these positions, not fully understanding the complexity of the skills required to be a successful shooter.

A GS and GA need to have a good awareness of space within the circle, as well as the ability to take control of that space and maintain focus on a consistent shooting action while under pressure from the defence. Never under-estimate the value of shooting practice!

In all the shooting drills to follow there are some key coaching points to consider and skills to encourage. For example:

- Shooters only have 3 seconds to turn and shoot, so the first thing to be sure of is correct balance. Without this, success will be limited. Feet should be shoulder width apart and toes should be pointing towards the net before attempting to make a shot.
- The power and energy for the shot comes from the ground so knees should be bent as if about to jump into the air. The back should be straight with the head up.
- The ball should be held on the fingertips above the head, supported by the other hand – not out in front of the player. The grip should be light, just enough to propel the ball into the net.
- Shooters should try to focus on a point at the back rather than the front of the ring, aiming high for the back of the net. Even if the shot is short, it could still fall in!
- Shooters should aim right before taking the shot and bend their elbows and knees when ready to shoot.
- The ball should be released at the same time as the shooter straightens her legs, moving the arms as little as possible but using a flick of the wrist to add backspin.
- As the shooter prepares to release the ball, she should drop her hands back behind her head. This is the most accurate way to control the direction of the ball.
- The shot should end with the shooter standing on tiptoes with the arms following through towards the ring.

Finally, always remember the golden rule in the circle for both attackers and defenders: always follow the shot in case it misses – rebounds represent a second chance! Take every opportunity to reaffirm this and form good habits.

drill 75 shooting skills

Objective: To practise shooting.

Equipment: Goalpost and a good supply of balls.

Description: Players stand facing the goalpost, feet parallel and shoulder width apart, holding the ball on the fingers of one hand directly above the head with a high, extended arm position, elbow close to the ear and pointing towards the ring. The fingers of the non-shooting hand are just used to support the ball. The shooting wrist should drop back slightly behind the head while the knees bend. Drive up with the legs and release the ball from just above the head with a flick of the wrist, following through to the target with the fingers. This wrist 'snap' gives the ball backspin and allows the ball to travel in a higher arc, increasing the chances of success.

Coaching points: Ask the shooter where she is aiming, what she sees, hears and feels when the ball goes well.

Progression: At the edge of the circle with their back to the goalpost, players throw the ball over their head, turn and catch it, then shoot.

drill 76 rolling attack

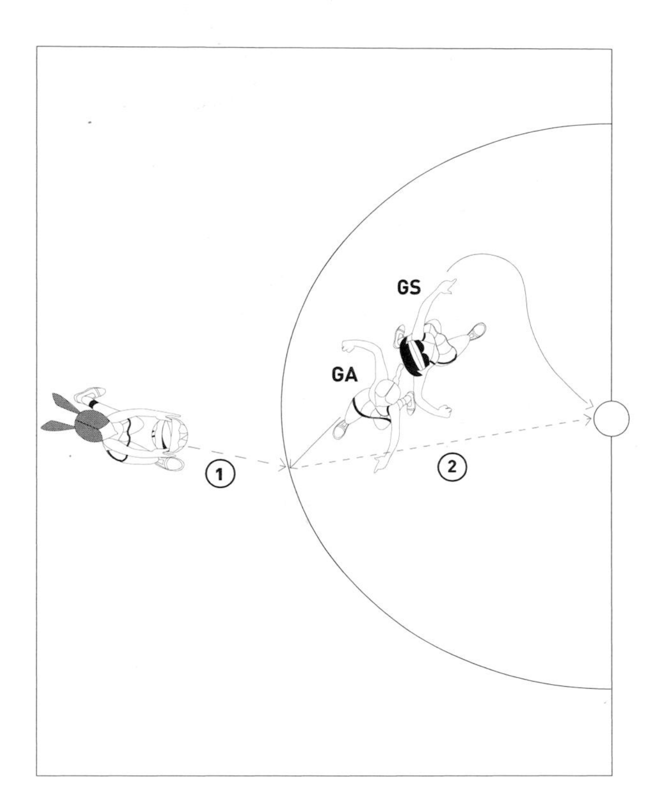

Objective: To improve communication between GA and GS.

Equipment: One ball and a goalpost between three players.

Description: Start off with GA and GS together in the heart of the circle. GA runs to receive a pass at the edge of the circle while GS 'rolls' off around the (imaginary) defender to take up a shooting position at the post. GA passes to GS, who shoots.

Coaching points: GS will be able to see what space GA takes up and should respond accordingly. Ensure that all movements are decisive and strong.

Progression: The first pass can be received at different points of the circle, and GS has to respond accordingly. Once the drill has been mastered add a defender.

drill 77 dirty dungeons

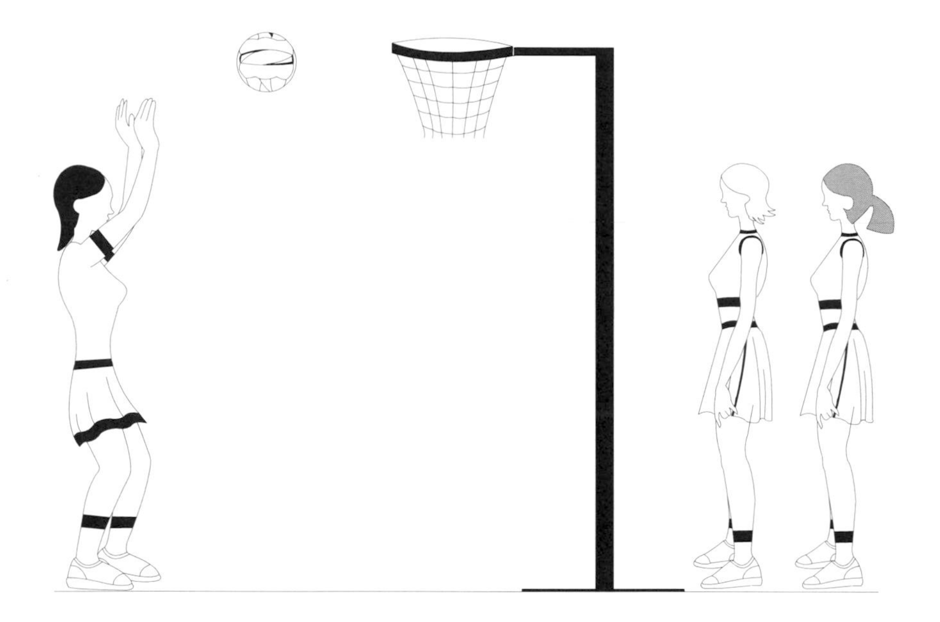

Objective: To practise shooting skills.

Equipment: A goalpost and two balls.

Description: Divide the players into two teams. Each team has one ball. Each player gets one shot in turn. If they are successful, they stay in the game; if they miss they must stand in the 'dungeon' (next to the post). Any player standing in the dungeon can be released back into the game by one of their team scoring a goal. When everybody on one team is in the dungeon, the other team wins.

Coaching points: Look for correct shooting action from a balanced position.

Progression: Add a defender.

drill 78 twenty-one

Objective: To practise shooting and going for the rebound.

Equipment: A goalpost and two balls.

Description: Divide the players into two teams. Each team has one ball. Each player has a shot for goal; if she is successful her team is awarded two points. If she catches the first shot on the rebound, she can have a second shot. The team is awarded one point for a successful second shot. The first team to 21 points is the winner. The team needs to win the game with a two-point shot regardless of their overall score.

Coaching points: This drill can be simplified for younger players by providing a target for them to aim a pass at, rather than shooting at goal.

Progression: Add a defender.

drill 79 shooting relay

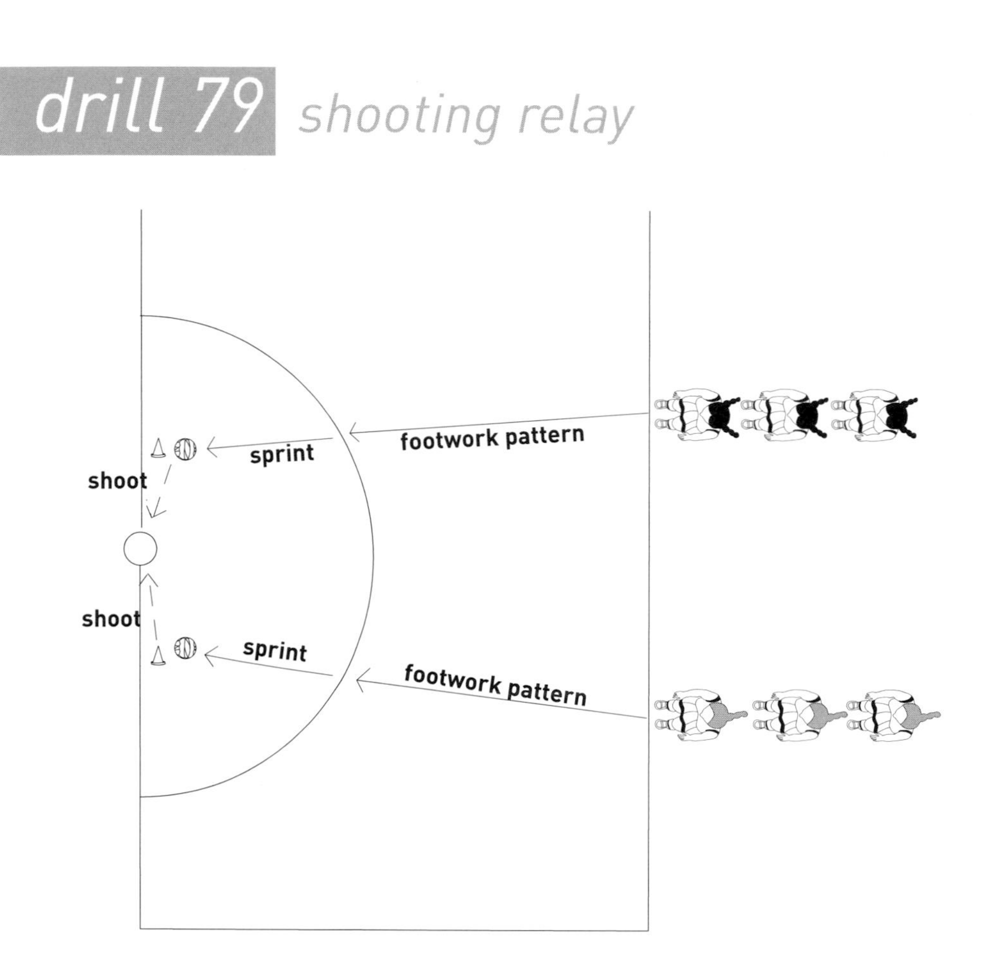

Objective: To practise getting into a balanced position to shoot following a move into the circle.

Equipment: Two balls, two cones and one goalpost. Players in two teams.

Description: The balls are placed at the cones, which are placed in the circle in a good shooting position. One at a time from each team, players move towards the circle edge using different movement patterns. They then sprint to the cone, pick up the ball and either score a goal or have a maximum of three shots at goal.They then pass the ball to the next player on their team, who should have reached the circle edge and then sprinted into the circle to receive the pass. The first player goes to the back of their team. Each player needs to complete three trips to the post. The first team to finish is the winner.

Coaching points: Look for balanced, controlled movement into the circle and a balanced shooting action.

Progression: Add a defender. Add a feeder to pass the ball to the shooters.

drill 80 rebound

Objective: To develop awareness and control of space in the circle.

Equipment: One ball between three players in the shooting circle.

Description: Two shooters stand in the circle. The feeder stands on the circle edge with the ball. The shooters dodge to get free and the feeder passes to each one in turn. The shooter then assumes a good shooting position and makes the shot, following the ball. The second shooter takes control of the space under the post, waiting for the rebound and preventing her imaginary defender from gaining access to this vital space. Shooters score one point for every successful shot and two points for every rebound caught. After each shot or rebound the ball is returned to the feeder.

Coaching points: Look for confident dodges into space and shooters holding space to receive a pass. Shooters should aim to receive the pass close to the post. Encourage shooters to follow every shot with their hands ready to catch the rebound.

Progression: Add defenders to mark the shooters. The feeder may choose to pass to whichever shooter is in the best position.

Alison Broadbent (the Swifts, Australia) defends against Eloise Southby (the Phoenix, Australia). Note the close marking and the contest for the ball.

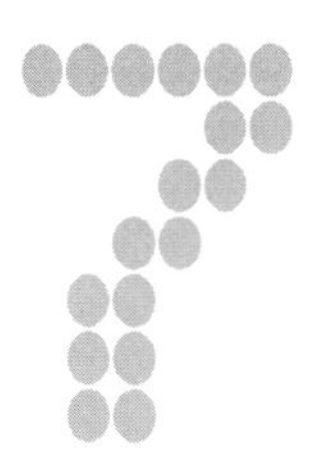

CONDITIONED GAMES

Conditioned games (CGs) are where players and coaches alike have the opportunity to put what they have practised into game situations. They are an excellent way to draw together the various skills that have been practised in drills.

For these 'matches' to be fully effective, the coach must ensure that the objective and the link between the drill and the game are very clear and fully understood by all the players. The players must be certain of the progression from drill to CG. Without this, this section will become a bit of a run-around at the end of the session instead of being a key learning opportunity. The best way to communicate this is to ask the players to identify the relevance of the drill themselves, for example 'where in a match do you think that you might see this situation?'

The most common mistake coaches make is to allow conditioned games to run for too long and to therefore digress from the key coaching element. A CG is intended to isolate a specific scenario or skill; by letting the game run on too long, more and more variables develop and the focus is lost.

Run the CG for a little while, then stop it and discuss (briefly) what has happened to reaffirm what the players are supposed to be practising, then recommence. Continue with this play–coach–play rhythm to ensure that the objectives and skills are ingrained.

Keep the CG sessions very short and sharp (3–5 minutes each at most) and keep the groups small even if this means you have to have two matches going at one time.

drill 81 half-court attacking game

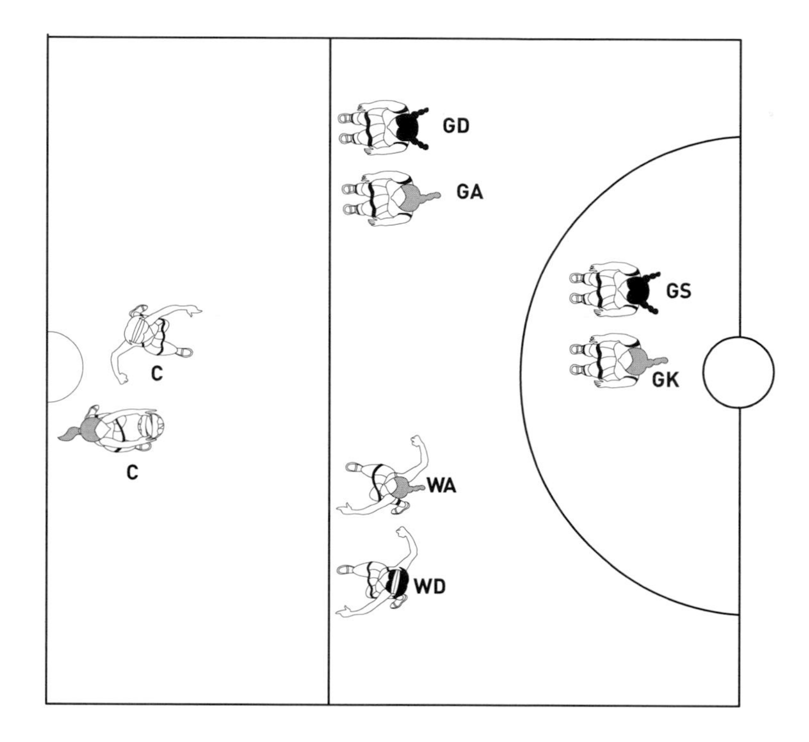

Area: Half court.

Players: Four-a-side.

Description: One team starts as the attackers, the other team are defenders. Starting with a centre pass, any player can shoot but only two are allowed in the circle at any time. If there is an interception the roles immediately change – attackers become defenders and vice versa. All netball rules apply. If three players enter the circle at the same time the roles change over and play re-starts with a new centre pass.

Coaching points: This drill encourages much greater movement by the shooters and widens their range of skills. Because of the circle restriction plenty of communication is required.

drill 82 free movement game

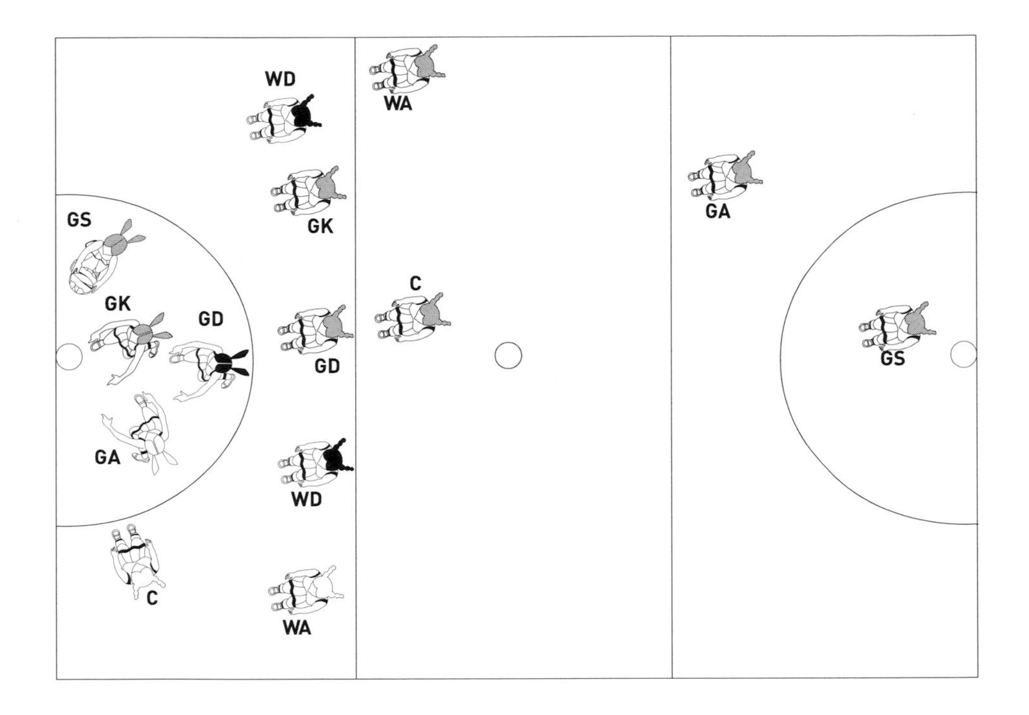

Area: Full court.

Players: Full teams.

Description: All outfield players can range freely outside the circle. For a goal to count, all players must be in the goal third at the time it is scored. Once a goal is scored the ball is immediately live.

Coaching points: This game opens up space on the court and involves lots of running. It is very frenetic so keep the sessions short and sharp. Frequent breaks allow recovery and also stop the game dissolving into a farce!

drill 83 two-ball game

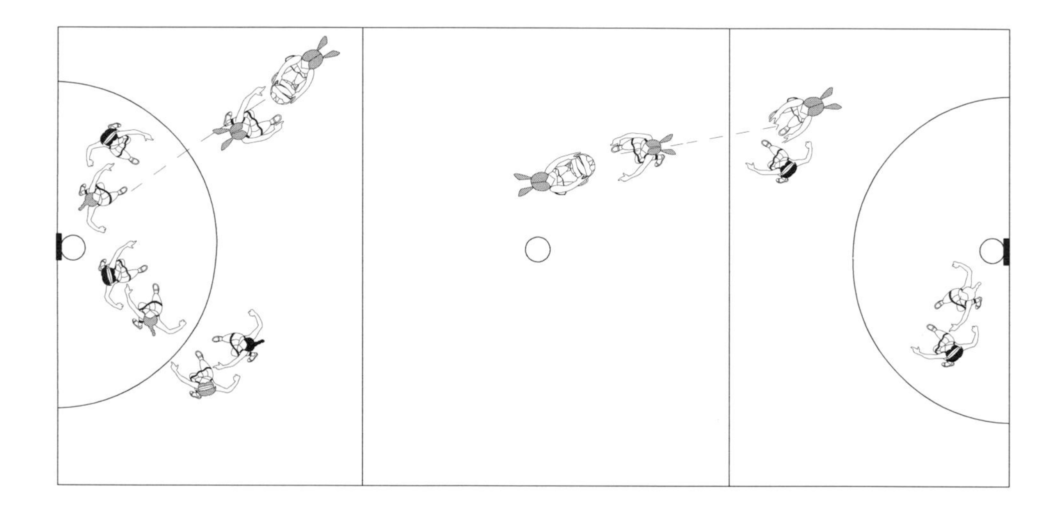

Area: Full court.

Players: Full teams.

Description: Play a normal game but introduce a second ball.

Coaching points: This makes sure that everyone is very awake! There is no restriction on a team having both balls at once, but be strict on the three-second possession rule. It might help to have two umpires!

drill 84 defence game

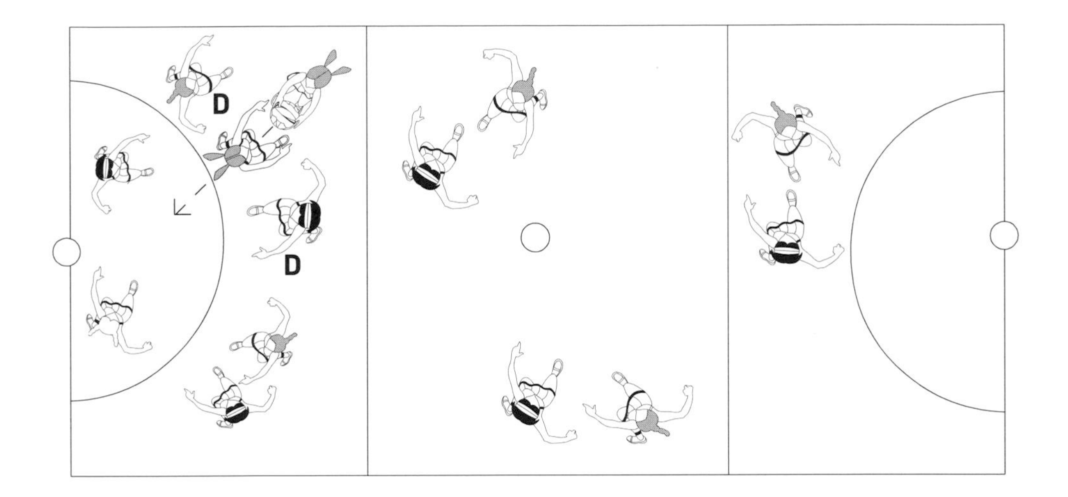

Area: Full court.

Players: Five-a-side with two extra defenders.

Description: Play a normal game, but introduce two players (without bibs) who are always defending and can roam the court freely outside the goal circles (Ds). GS and GK are absent from each team and only GA and GD are permitted in the circle. All other players can roam freely.

Coaching points: Rotate the defenders every three minutes as this is a real lung-buster. Look for all defenders marking the ball with arms high, and definite dodges to get free by the attackers.

drill 85 bounce-pass game

Area: Half court.

Players: Six-a-side (no GS or GK).

Description: Play a standard game but the only pass allowed is a bounce pass. If the ball bounces more than once, possession is lost immediately to the other team. Allow three minutes per team then stop the drill for two minutes to allow the players to recover.

Coaching points: As the bounce pass can only travel a short distance, this drill will make attackers and defenders alike work very hard.

drill 86 attacking practice

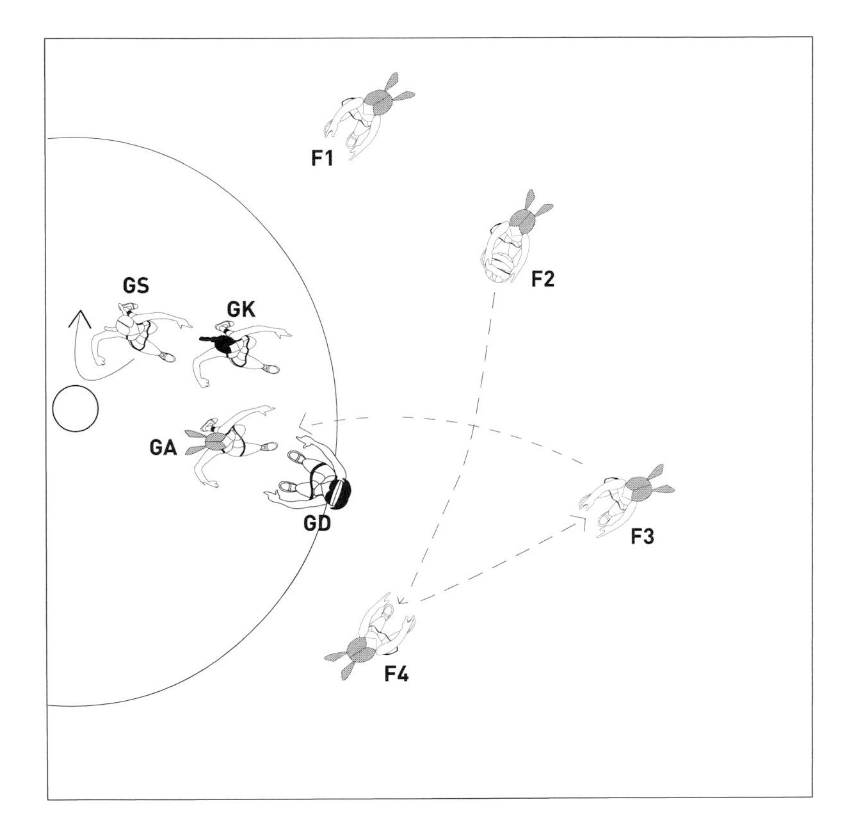

Area: Goal third.

Players: Two against two, plus four feeders with one ball each.

Description: The objective is to work the circle players hard. The feeders (F1–4) stand 1 m back from the circle with a ball on the floor behind them. All the feeders are attackers and pass one ball around them looking for the best feed in. The GK and GD have to defend for as long as possible to stop first the feed and then the shot. Once the GS or GA has shot (successfully or not) the feeders re-start with another ball.

Coaching points: Feeders must complete three passes before each feed. The GS and GA will need to make quick, definite dodges both within the circle and moving out into the goal third to create space and get free from their defender.

drill 87 silent game

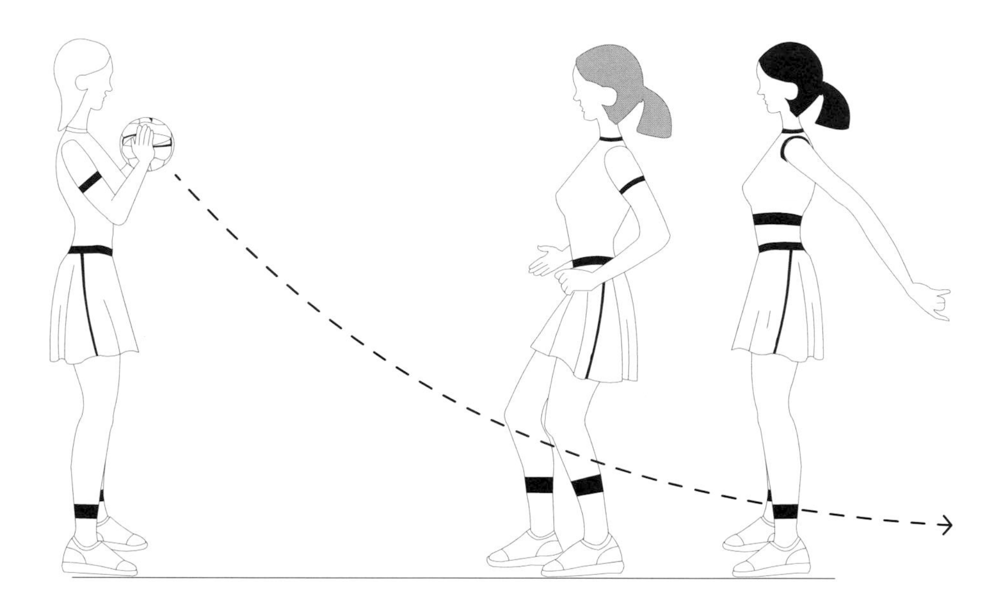

Area: Full court.

Players: Full teams.

Description: Play a normal game, but no talking or calling is allowed. Players must use hand and eye signals only.

Coaching points: Use this game sparingly. It is particularly useful if a team is not good at communicating. Removing verbal communication temporarily will emphasise its importance. Run the game for five minutes and then, during recovery, invite the comments of the players. Was it easier or more difficult without words? Does signalling have any advantages at all?

drill 88 driving to the pass

Area: Full court.

Players: Full teams.

Description: Play a normal game, but players are only allowed to receive a pass by driving onto the ball. Apart from that all rules apply. You may need to be a bit more lenient on the three-second rule until players become accustomed to the drill.

Coaching points: As fatigue sets in, a common issue is for players to drift away from the ball or not move at all. This drill seeks to address this problem by asking the players to put themselves in a position to drive onto the pass. Occasionally, players will have to move away from the ball to give themselves enough room to drive into, but always insist on the receiver moving dynamically in.

drill 89 centre spacing

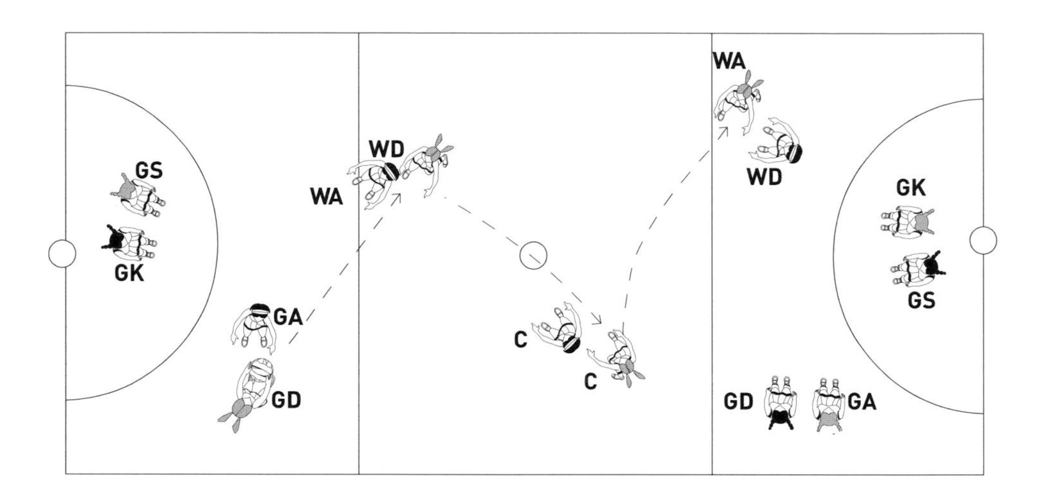

Area: Full court.

Players: Full teams.

Description: Play a normal game, but GA and GD must not come out of the goal third. This is a good game if spacing is an issue (particularly with younger, inexperienced players).

Coaching points: Use this drill as an opportunity for C, WA and WD to develop their use of the extra space.

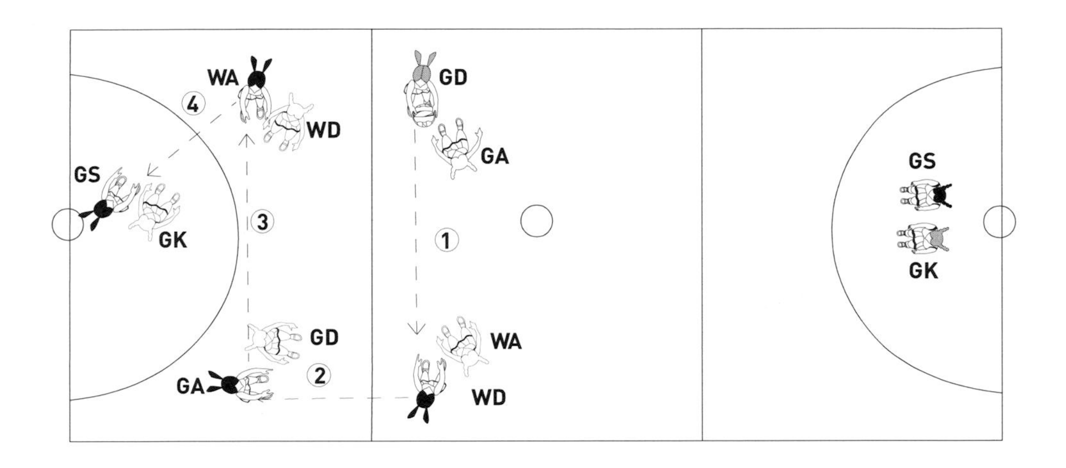

Area: Full court.

Players: Full teams.

Description: Play a normal game, but players are not allowed to return a pass to the same player that passed to them. This is a good drill when teams struggle to develop space.

Coaching points: This game forces players to find space, but if they are finding it too easy then remove a player. This will then give only four options to the passer.

drill 91 shooters showtime

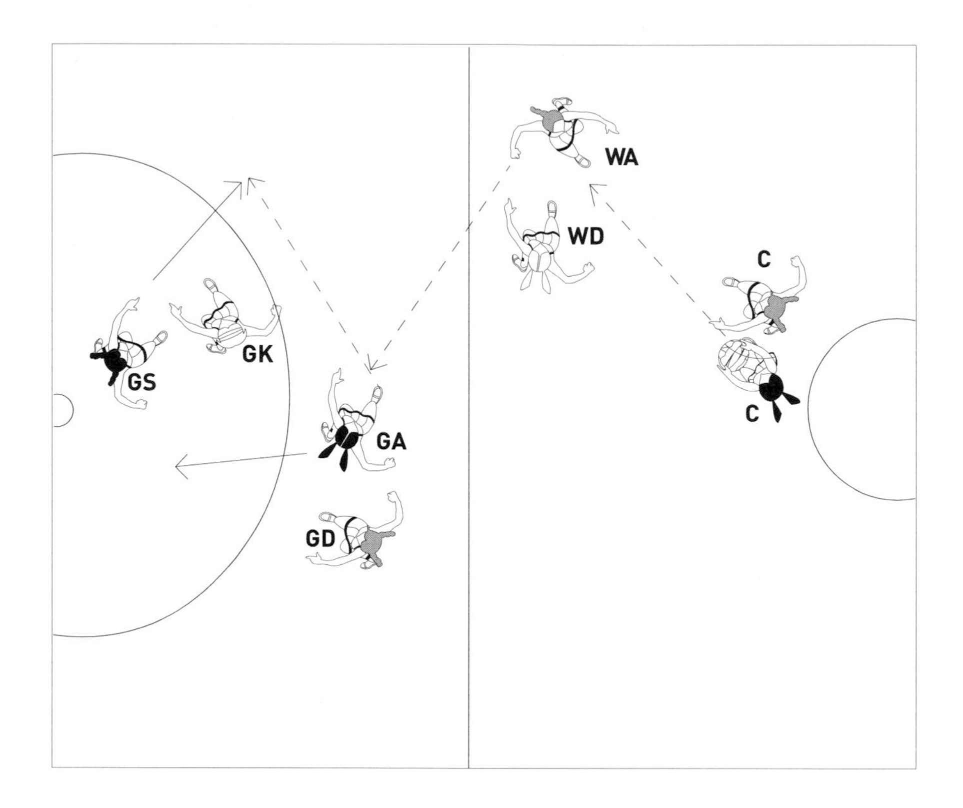

Area: Half court.

Players: Half teams (C, WA, GA, GS againt C, WD, GD, GK).

Description: Begin play from a centre pass every time the game is re-started. A goal only counts if the GS has taken a pass outside the circle before the goal is scored.

Coaching points: This forces the GS to move and stops her from loitering under the post waiting for the ball. Be careful that the GA does not in turn become lazy.

the centre pass

The following drills will help players practise good technique at the centre pass. The starting position at each centre pass is crucial for the attacking players. The WA and GA should try to get into a position along the third line they are happy with, preferably on the outside of their defending player. Standing too close to the side line restricts the space for the players to run into to receive the pass, but if the WA and GA stand too close together in the centre of the third line it makes it easy for the defenders to mark them and stop the attackers' run to receive the pass. Defenders WD and GD should try to make things as difficult for their attacking partners as possible by dominating the space along the third line, forcing the WA and GA to take up a position that is easier to mark and reduces the space available for them to run into.

drill 92 attacking centre pass

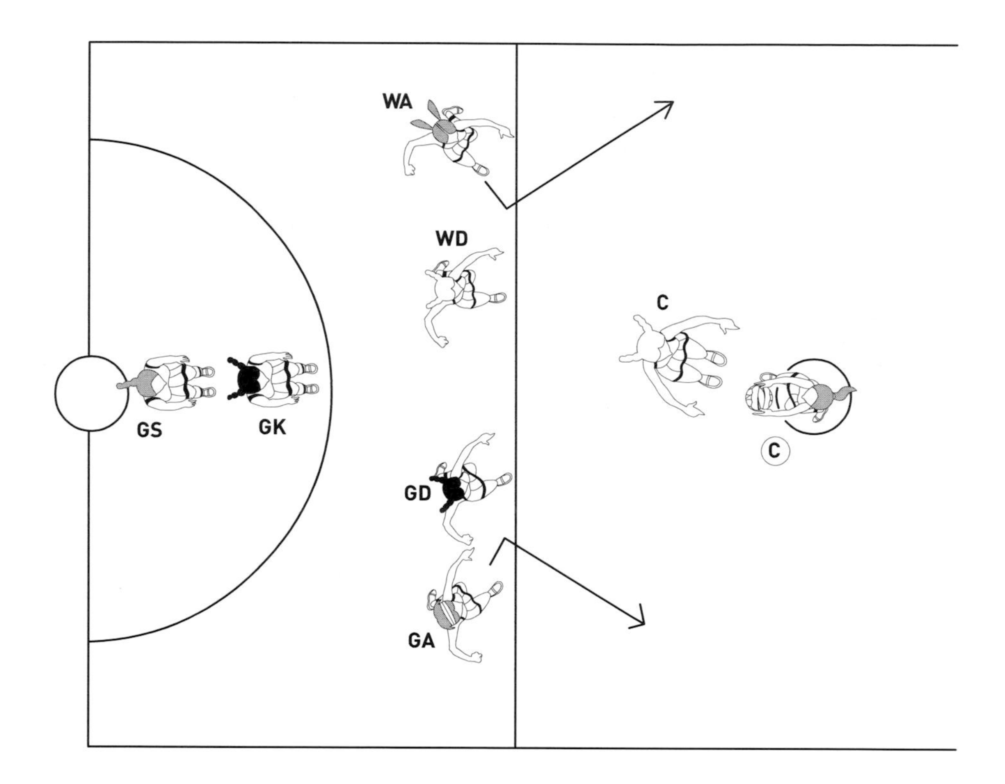

Objective: To practise dodging to get free and receive the centre pass.

Equipment: One ball and the half court between eight players.

Description: This drill allows players to practise an alternative way of getting free for the centre pass than a simple straight run to the side. On the coach's whistle, the WA and GA dodge to get free and sprint into the centre third. The defenders should stand still at first. The pass can go to either player, as chosen by the C (for younger players the coach may need to indicate where the pass should go at first).

Coaching points: The dodge should be a definite movement: controlled, quick and balanced. Look for the WA and GA pushing off on their outside foot and using their shoulders to help feign the dodge and make the move quick and controlled.

Progression: Introduce the defenders. Encourage them to try to stick with their attacking partners and intercept the ball.

drill 93 centre pass using WD and GD

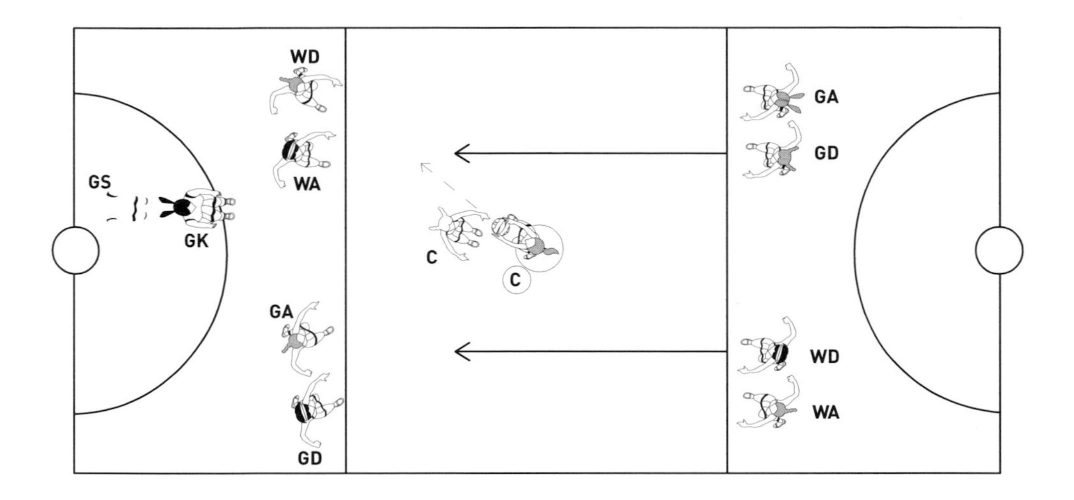

Objective: To practise WD/GD receiving a centre pass in an attacking position.

Equipment: One ball and half the court between twelve players.

Description: Set up the players as shown. C starts with the ball and should be facing away from the WD and GD. On the coach's whistle, WD and GD sprint forwards in a straight line, aiming to receive the ball as close to the attacking third line as possible. Alternate the players receiving the pass. Restrict defending players (WA and GA) until the WD and GD are more confident.

Coaching points: To receive a centre pass without the ball being intercepted, the WD and GD should position themselves inside their defending players ready for the centre pass. It is worth letting WD and GD try to receive the centre pass having started on the outside of their defending players – this puts the C under more pressure to make an accurate pass and makes it easier for WA and GA to intercept the ball.

Progression: Encourage the defending players to try for the interception. Look for the player receiving the pass to make a second pass to either the WA or GA.

the throw-in

The next set of drills will help develop good technique when taking and receiving throw-ins from various positions on court. Who takes the throw-in depends on where on the court the ball goes out of play. The following drills show typical positions for a throw-in on the court. Younger players don't always think about positioning and spacing on court and are keen to take throw-ins to be part of the game wherever they may be. However, if the player taking the throw-in is out of position on the court, this can have a negative impact on the next sequence of passes in the game. Encouraging young players to think about the 'correct' person to take the throw-in is a good habit to get into.

The following drills enable players to practise set moves for a variety of throw-ins, although the combinations are endless and players will need to be encouraged to be flexible and think about the best options available in each situation.

Coaching points to consider when taking a throw-in

1. When taking a throw-in, the player must stand with one foot up to – but not touching – the line of the court. This indicates to the umpire that the player is ready to make the pass. If the player's feet are touching the line, a free throw-in will be given to the opposite team. An umpire may also penalise a player who is standing too far away from the line – this is not likely to happen with younger players, but good positioning is a good habit to get into.
2. The player taking the throw-in should look to pass the ball into an attacking or forward position on court. There may be occasions when the throw-in will need to be passed backwards if players are not free, but players should be encouraged to look forwards.
3. All players must be on court before the pass is taken. This also applies to members of the opposite team, who may have gone off court to retrieve the ball. If a player takes the throw-in without waiting for that player to be on court, a free pass will be given to the opposite team.
4. Players on court should be ready to receive the pass, either holding a space to run into or ready to dodge and get free.
5. Players defending a throw-in should be 1 m away from the line to avoid giving away a penalty pass.
6. Any back line throw-in taken in the defence goal third should be taken by the GK.
7. Never throw a back line pass across the circle – if the pass is intercepted, this gives the attacking team an immediate shot at goal.

The player taking the throw-in can decide whether to take the throw-in quickly or take more time. There may be an advantage gained if the throw-in is taken quickly – for example to get the ball into the circle to an unmarked GA or GS. There may also be advantages to taking more time to prepare before taking the throw-in – for example if team players are out of position and need time to recover on court.

drill 94 throw-in from the back line – in the circle

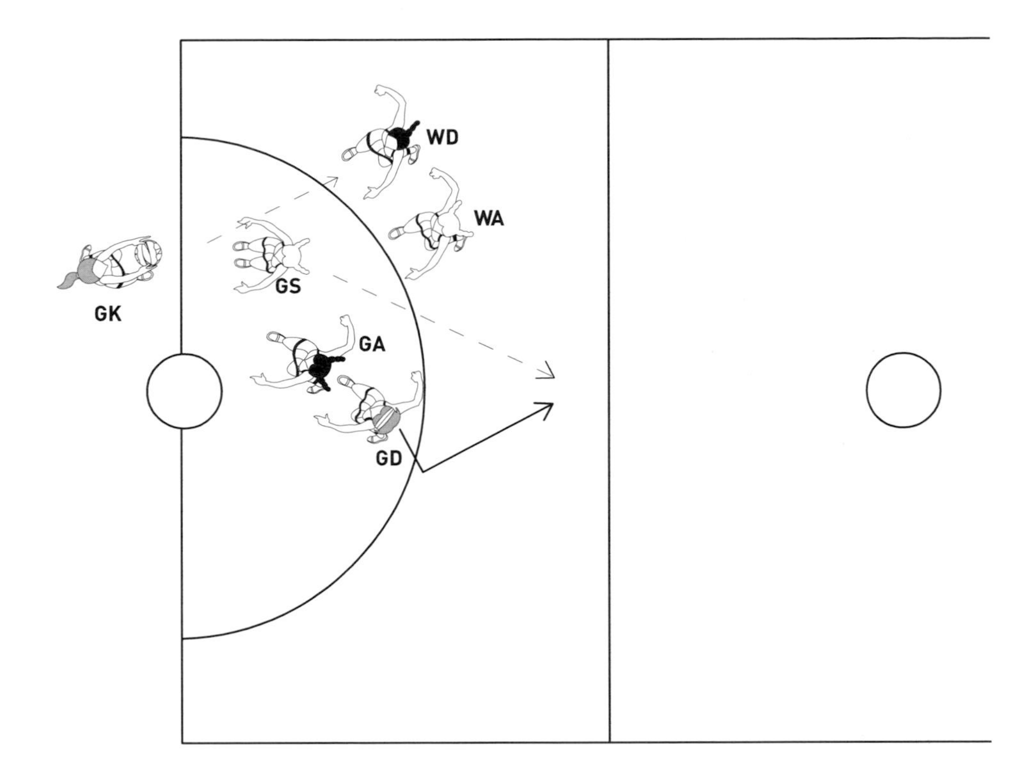

Objective: To practise WD and GD receiving a back line throw-in in the circle.

Equipment: One ball and half the court between five players.

Description: The defensive back line pass will always be taken by the GK, whereever the ball goes out of court. The GK starts with the ball standing on the backline. The other players start in the positions shown. WD and GD hold their position on the circle edge – making it harder for the WA and GA to mark them. When ready, the GK should step up to the line as if to take the throw-in, which is the indication to the other players that she/he is ready. The WD or GD is going to receive the pass at the circle edge, shielding the ball from the WA or GA with her body. Alternatively, the WD or GD can dodge to get free. Alternate passes to WD and GD.

Coaching points: Encourage the WD and GD to hold the space on the edge of the circle. Any movement before the pass will give an advantage to the defender.

Progression: The GD or WD – depending on who receives the first ball – should be ready for the next pass.

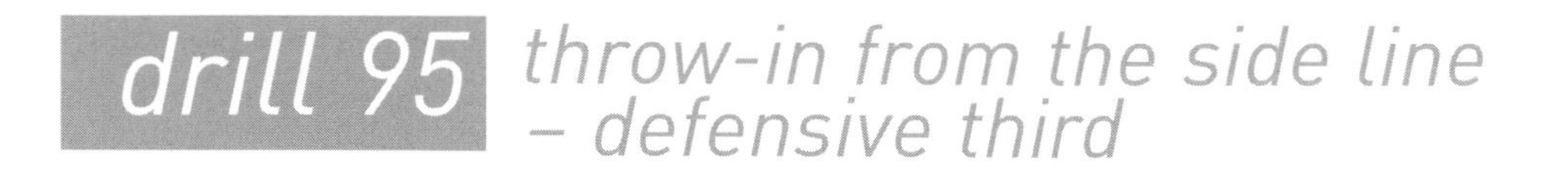

drill 95 throw-in from the side line – defensive third

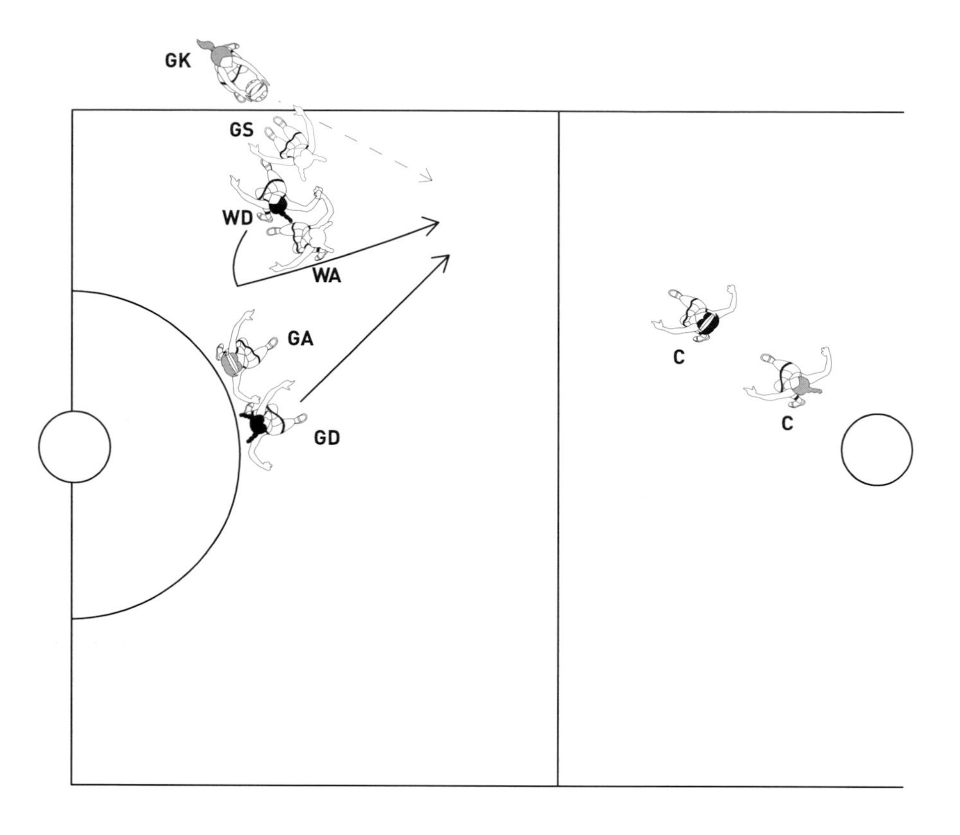

Objective: To practise a side line throw-in in the defensive third.

Equipment: One ball and half the court between five players.

Description: The GK should take the throw-in. The WD or GD should aim to receive the pass. WD and GD should dodge to get free of their marker or hold a space to run into. Alternate passes to WD and GD. If WD receives the throw-in, the GD should move for the next pass and vice versa.

Coaching points: Encourage communication between the players. Players should hold their space and resist moving up the court to help receive the pass – this causes crowding.

Progression: The GK decides which player to pass to depending on who is in the best position to receive the pass.

drill 96 throw-in from the side line – centre court

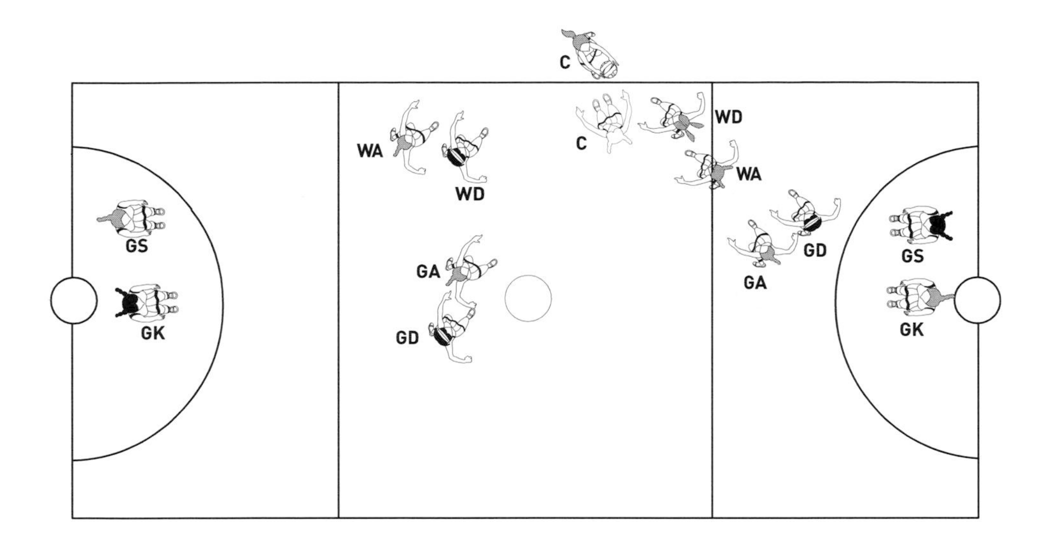

Objective: To practise a throw-in in the centre court. The aim is to encourage players to decide who will receive the throw-in and avoid crowding around the ball.

Equipment: One ball and the full court.

Description: The coach should vary the position of the throw-in. Let the players play out the side line pass aiming to maintain an attacking position.

Coaching points: The coach must ensure that a clear pass is given to a player and that the player receiving the throw-in makes a definite move to receive the ball. Other players should avoid crowding and look to receive the next pass. Encourage lots of communication and stop the drill if players do crowd the ball. Walk the players through the possible moves if needed.

Progression: Vary the player taking the throw-in and receiving the pass. Encourage the players to take responsibility for deciding who will take the throw-in and receive the pass rather than the coach dictating this all the time.

England GS Louisa Bradfield demonstrates the strength and agility needed when jumping to receive a pass to avoid the defending player making an interception. Although Louisa's height gives her an advantage as GS, on this occasion it is her ability to jump and maintain balance that has given her the edge over her defender.

8

WARMING DOWN

At the end of the session the players will be hot and probably tired. It is a mistake to just say, 'Thanks for coming' and let them wander off. Instead, always perform a warm-down to finish each session. This will provide a number of important functions:

- The warm-down is a great opportunity to work on flexibility as the muscles are warm.
- The warm-down allows the body to begin to flush out many of the waste products produced during vigorous exercise.
- The warm-down represents the 'bracket' to the session and will ensure that players feel that this was a well-thought-out, well-structured session, which all adds to the atmosphere of excellence and care that will motivate a group to work effectively.

Just as with all the drills in this book, the warm-down sessions must focus on form; only strict form will provide the intended benefits.

drill 97 hamstring reach

Objective: To warm down the body and to improve flexibility.

Equipment: One ball per player.

Description: Line the players up along the base line with feet wider than shoulder width apart and the ball between their feet. On the coach's command, the players reach down (keeping their legs straight at all times), pick up the ball and place it as far back through their legs as they can. The player then walks backwards until their feet are in line with the ball and repeats the drill. The aim is to cover the given distance (approximately 10 m) in as few pick-ups as possible.

Coaching points: Watch for cheats who bend their legs to gain an advantage! Remind them that this is a slow, controlled race and form is everything.

drill 98 side stretch

Objective: To warm down the body and improve flexibility.

Equipment: One ball per player.

Description: Line the players up with their right side facing into court, feet wider than shoulder width apart, legs straight and the ball in front of their left foot. On the coach's command, the players bend down (keeping their legs straight), pick up the ball and place it in front of their right foot. Then, leaving the ball where it is, the players swap feet, progressing into the court, so that the ball is by their left foot once more. The movement is then repeated for a set distance – 10 m is more than enough for this drill.

Coaching points: Watch for cheats who bend their legs to gain an advantage! Reiterate that the movements should be slow and controlled, keeping perfect form.

drill 99 circle stretch 1

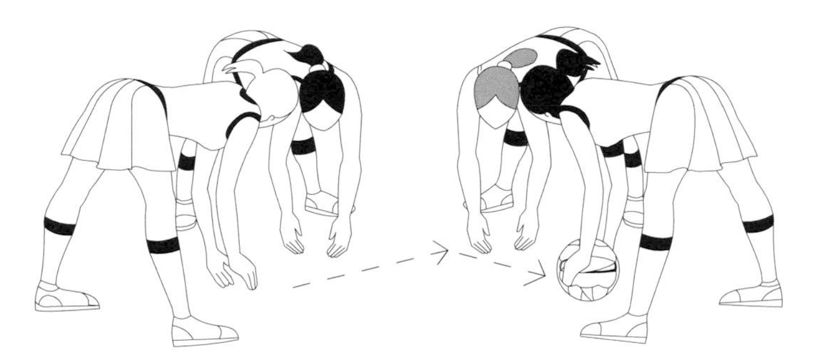

Objective: To warm down the body and improve flexibility.

Equipment: One ball between six players.

Description: Form the players into a circle with their feet wider than shoulder width apart, and their feet touching those of the next players (i.e. right foot to left foot). Keeping the legs straight, all the players reach down and hang their hands as close to the floor as possible. The ball is rolled from one player to another around the circle. After ten passes in total, walk the players around for a minute and then repeat.

Coaching points: Watch for cheats who bend their legs to gain an advantage!

Progression: If you have enough players, form two or more groups and race them to see who is first to complete the passes.

drill 100 circle stretch 2

Objective: To warm down the body and improve flexibility.

Equipment: One ball between six players.

Description: Sit the players back to back in a circle with their legs wide apart and feet touching. The ball is passed in order around the circle. Each player must give and take the ball with two hands every time.

Coaching points: This drill provides a stretch to the backs of the legs and requires good flexibility, as each player must rotate the trunk to make the pass. If players lack flexibility, they will creep their bottoms away from the group so that they are leaning back rather than sitting upright. Try to keep the legs nice and straight throughout.

Progression: If you have enough players, form two or more groups and race to see who is the first to complete the passes. Vary the direction of passing on command.

drill 101 giant strides

Objective: To warm down the body and improve flexibility.

Equipment: Cones.

Description: Players line up facing into court. Mark out a line about 10 m away using the cones. Keeping the body upright, each player takes a slow, controlled stride forwards. The stride should be as long as possible without losing control. Repeat over the set distance then walk the players back to the start. Repeat.

Coaching points: This drill only works if the body is strictly upright with a 'proud' chest and the head up. In effect, it is an exaggerated running stride. The more slowly this drill is performed, the better. The challenge is for each player to beat her own standards – if she can cover the distance in five strides, she should try to cover it in four and a half next time, and so on.